I0053850

Data Architecture

Building the Foundation

Bill Inmon
Dave Rapien

Technics Publications
SEDONA, ARIZONA

TECHNICS PUBLICATIONS

115 Linda Vista, Sedona, AZ 86336 USA
https://www.TechnicsPub.com

Edited by Steve Hoberman
Cover design by Lorena Molinari

All rights reserved. No part of this book may be reproduced or transmitted in any form or by any means, electronic or mechanical, including photocopying, recording or by any information storage and retrieval system, without written permission from the publisher, except for brief quotations in a review.

The authors and publisher have taken care in the preparation of this book but make no expressed or implied warranty of any kind and assume no responsibility for errors or omissions. No liability is assumed for incidental or consequential damages in connection with or arising out of the use of the information or programs contained herein.

All trade and product names are trademarks, registered trademarks, or service marks of their respective companies and are the property of their respective holders and should be treated as such.

Without in any way limiting the author's exclusive rights under copyright, any use of this publication to "train" generative artificial intelligence (AI) technologies to generate text is expressly prohibited. The author reserves all rights to license uses of this work for generative AI training and the development of machine learning language models.

First Printing 2025

Copyright © 2025 by Bill Inmon and Dave Rapien

ISBN, print ed.   9781634626354
ISBN, Kindle ed.   9781634626361
ISBN, PDF ed.   9781634626385

Contents

Preface

Every few years, the high-tech industry comes up with a new technology. Recently, there has been machine learning (ML), artificial intelligence (AI), and data mesh. In years past, it was .com, big data, and data science. Before that, a host of other technologies.

Each of these new technologies has its own appeal and promise. However, as new technologies emerge, they all start with the same basic assumption. That assumption is that there is a firm foundation of data in the corporation on which to operate.

The truth is that there is *not* a firm foundation of data in the corporation on which to operate. For many reasons, data within the corporation is fractured and unreliable. Yet the successful adoption and operation of these new technologies depend on this basic fact.

The inability of new technologies to succeed can be stated simply as one of the oldest truths in technology: GIGO (garbage in, garbage out).

Stated differently, if these new technologies lack a credible foundation of data on which to operate, they will fail to meet the corporation's needs and ultimately be unsuccessful.

Building on the foundation of data to make new technologies successful is not an easy task. It is a long-term, ongoing activity.

Building that foundation requires a skill set that most technicians lack. That skill set builds on architecture, not technology.

No magic button can be pushed that makes the architecture suddenly appear.

Instead, building and maintaining an architecture is a long-term task accomplished a day at a time, a step at a time.

Building and maintaining a data architecture begins with an understanding of what that architecture needs to look like. Data architecture, like all other architectures, has a definite set of guidelines and propositions that shape it. You can recognize data architecture very distinctly.

In this book, you will find important topics such as:

- Data integration and transformation
- Structured data
- Textual data
- Analog data
- Data catalog
- Data lineage
- Data quality
- Data architect
- Data architecture evolution

And these are just a few of the many subjects covered in the book.

To achieve success with new technology, you must have a solid foundation on which to build.

This book describes the shape and shaping factors of data architecture.

It sets the stage for success.

Bill Inmon/Denver, Colorado
Dave Rapien/Cincinnati, Ohio

.

Chapter 1

The Solid Foundation of Data for New Technologies

Every day, new technology is announced. Since technology has become an integral part of business, vendors and entrepreneurs have continually developed new ways to make technology more useful and cost-effective.

In recent years, several new and powerful technologies have become available. As new technologies become more powerful and sophisticated, there has been an increasing reliance on the underlying data on which these technologies operate. Simply stated, the new technologies need a foundation of corporate data on which to operate.

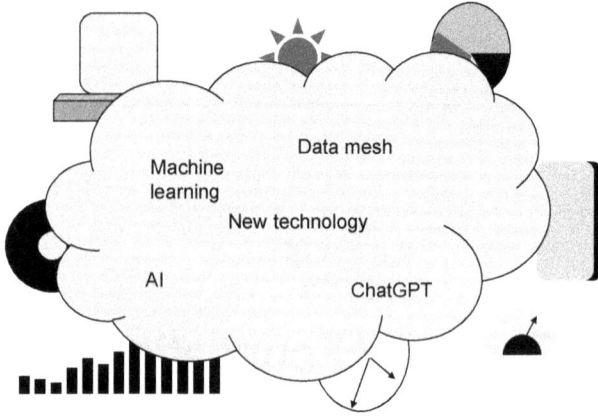

Figure 1: New technologies rely on a foundation of data to operate properly.

A problem

In every case where new technologies rely on an underlying foundation of data, a problem arises. The problem is that new technologies are no better or more effective than the data on which they operate.

Only a handful of organizations have a solid foundation of underlying data on which to operate. Data has accumulated over the years in a variety of ways. Many vendors, offering various types and formats of data, have contributed to the growing pile of data that organizations have. In almost every case, the data that has accumulated was never designed to work with data from other vendors. In other cases, the application designer did not include all the needed data. In another case, the application designer treated the data incorrectly. In yet another case, a vendor was replaced with another vendor. Finally, data was collected for one purpose and then used for another purpose.

In another scenario, the foundation of data that exists in the corporation today is not wrong, but it is misleading. Applications were built to solve the business problems of a corporation at one point in time. Over time, businesses change. There is a merger. There is a new product line. There is new competition. There is a change in economic conditions. There is new legislation. For various reasons, the corporation's business is constantly evolving. The applications written and the data collected at one point in time are simply not useful or relevant at a later time. Attempting to revisit and utilize data from an earlier moment in time may yield very misleading results.

A foundation of sand

To use an analogy, if you build a house on a firm foundation of bedrock, it will stand. However, if you build your house on the sand of the beach, it will wash away with the tide or the first storm.

The truth is that most corporations have an unreliable foundation of data. The corporation's focus is on the latest, cutting-edge technology. The problem with the foundation of data is that the vendors, the trade press, and the conferences all focus elsewhere. No one is focusing on the foundational data that is needed to make new technologies operate correctly.

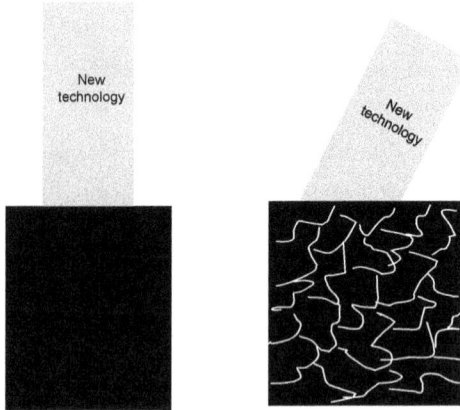

Figure 2: New technology placed on a foundation of sand will not succeed.

It takes hard work to go back into the foundation of data and reconstitute it properly. It is not glamorous to dig through old data and reconstitute it.

If you don't go back and reconstitute your existing data foundation, you will not be able to believe the results that your new technology comes up with, not with any great degree of confidence, at least. Reconstituting the existing foundation of data requires:

- **Finding and looking at old documentation**. Documentation was often never produced or maintained.

- **Digging meaning out of old programs**. The technology in which the old programs were written may not even exist today. The corporation may not even be able to hire personnel who understand the technology.

- **Finding and understanding the metadata that describes the existing foundation of data.** Such metadata may have been lost or is badly out of date.

- **Finding people who understand how older systems work.** In many cases, these people have long retired.

About data architecture

The solid foundation of data needed to support new technologies is built on data architecture. Data architecture is not a technology. Instead, data architecture is a conceptual foundation that can be expressed or embodied by one or more technologies (usually more). The five most important data architecture pillars are to support:

- **Business value.** If the architecture does not support significant business value, the data architecture will likely not endure for the long term. Technologies that do not provide genuine business value ultimately collapse.

- **Data transformation.** Data plays multiple roles within the corporation. To fulfill the roles that data needs to play, it must be transformed. As a simple example of the need for transformation, a corporation has reports of dollar revenue from its sources. One source is the USA. Another source is Canada. And a third source is

Australia. Although the revenue is reported in dollars, different exchange rates apply to each source. To be meaningful, the dollar values need to be transformed into a single, uniform dollar value. The need for transformation far surpasses exchange rate calculations and includes the transformation of data names, encoding conventions, calculations, and measurements.

- **Data model**. The world of data is large and complex. Many people need to examine and utilize data. The data model serves as a compass to guide users, developers, designers, analysts, and others through the morass of data. An organization without a data model is like a ship in the middle of the ocean without a compass. The ship is unlikely to see land again without a compass.

- **Definable architecture**. The fourth pillar of data architecture is the need for definable architecture. What are the components of the architecture? How can you tell the components of an architecture from anything else? How do the components of the architecture fit together? What shape and content do they have? Data architecture done correctly requires a recognizable and definitive explanation of what the architecture looks like, its components, and how those components behave.

- **Data types**. The fifth pillar of data architecture is that the architecture must encompass all of the different types of data encountered in the corporation. Data architecture must encompass structured, textual, and analog data. These three types of data are as different as the ocean, land, and the moon. The rules of survival in the sea are completely different from those on land. And living on the moon is entirely different than living on land or in the sea. Yet data architecture cannot restrict itself to the world of structured data, which most professionals are familiar with. Instead, the data architecture must encompass all types of data.

A solid foundation of data

There are many different elements and facets to the creation of a solid foundation of data. Furthermore, the elements of a solid foundation of data are widely diverse. Some facets deal with the accuracy of the data. Some facets deal with the naming and location of the data. Some facets deal with the creation of the data and its level of atomicity. These types and metadata properties are needed to build a solid foundation of usable data.

Accessibility of data

The most basic and obvious element of a solid foundation of data starts with the accessibility of data. If data is not accessible, it doesn't matter about anything else.

In the past, the accessibility of data meant being able to find the data in an electronic manner. There is still that need today. In this case, the programmer or analyst needs to be able to locate the data and access it efficiently. In today's world, data is often available electronically. The data is hiding behind an avalanche of other data. There is so much data that finding a given unit of data becomes a truly difficult and arduous task.

Metadata

One of the keys to data accessibility is the metadata that enables analysts to locate the data. If metadata exists and is accurate, the data in the foundation can be found. If metadata does not exist, finding data in the existing foundation is very difficult.

Lacking metadata about the existing foundation is like trying to drive from Florida to Seattle without a roadmap. When you take such a journey, you go through Maine, Pennsylvania, California, and back to Utah. Such a journey is simply nonsensical.

In the earliest days, the only kind of data was structured data. Metadata was certainly needed to find structured data. Typical forms of metadata were such things as:

- Database definitions
- File layouts
- Indexes and keys.

> *As other types of data emerged,*
> *metadata began to take on a different form.*

For example, in textual data, metadata takes the form of an ontology and/or a series of taxonomies (hierarchies of tags). In the case of analog data, metadata takes the form of the distillation algorithms that apply to the analog data.

Completeness

Another trait of a solid data foundation is the ability of the data collection to be complete. It does little good for data to exist in lots of little unrelated piles. Instead, the data needs to be integrated into a cohesive whole. This does not mean that there needs to be a single large physical database encompassing all the data. It is perfectly acceptable (and normal) for the data to physically reside in multiple places. All those places where the data resides need to be integrated into a cohesive network. It needs to be clear to the user what data is where, how it can be accessed, and how it relates to all the other data in the network.

Currency of data

Another element of a solid foundation of data is that it needs to be current. Data that is not current can be very misleading.

Currency of data means different things to different people. To the bank teller cashing a check, currency means the exact amount of money in a customer's account, up to the second. To the accountant calculating quarterly revenue, the currency of data means the accuracy of data for the quarter. To the manager making strategic decisions, currency means data that is accurate as of a year's ending.

Transaction-based data needs to be current up to the second. Other data needs to be current, depending on the nature of the data. Sometimes, data is current when it is a day old. Other data is current when it is a week old. The currency of the data depends entirely on the usage of the data and the data itself. In any case, data needs to be current in the solid foundation of data following the appropriate usage of the data.

Relatability of data

A very important element of a solid data foundation on which to support new technologies is the relatability of data. There are many disparate types of data found in the foundation. There are different definitions of data. There are different formats of data. There are different physical characteristics of data. There are different encodings of data. To do analytics on the data, different types of data must be able to be related. The relationships need to be accurate.

For example, a bank has a customer, John Jones, with a credit card. The bank has another customer, J Jones, II, with a loan. The bank needs to know if these two people are the same.

Unless the data can be related, there is no solid foundation of data.

Origins of data

An important aspect of the solid foundation of data needed to support new technology is a description of the origins of data. On many occasions, the analyst who needs to use the data needs to know the origins of the data so they can verify its validity and the appropriateness of its use.

As an example, the analyst is looking at revenue. Does the revenue include taxes paid at the moment of purchase or not? Does the revenue amount take into account foreign and domestic revenue? What exactly does revenue mean? The best way to discover what is meant by revenue is to go back to the source system and discover the meaning of those terms.

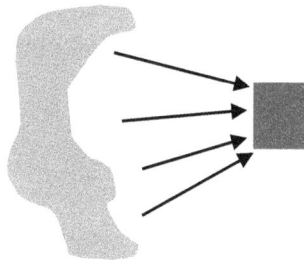

Figure 3: The source of the data in the foundation is clearly identified.

Naming conventions

The names of data in an earlier world include such things as:

- Database name
- Attribute name
- Index name.

In a more modern world, the data names include:

- Taxonomies
- Ontologies
- Context.

The names that data has assumed help everyone to know what data is being dealt with. There is a long list of people that good names help, including the:

- Analyst
- End user
- Programmer
- Manager
- Designer.

The acid test for proper naming of data is that there is a clear and unambiguous name for the data found in the foundation. For example, the name "xt-23a" says nothing about the type of data being represented. The name is simply nondescriptive. Examples of more descriptive names are Customer, Social Security Number, Gender, and Part Number.

Accuracy

Of course, the data that is found in the foundation should be accurate. If the data found in the foundation is not accurate, then the new technology that uses the data cannot also be accurate. For example, poor business decisions may be made if an account has been closed but the data indicates it is still open.

Atomicity of data

To aid clarity, the data in the foundation must be stored at the most atomic level. Data can be summarized and derived in the foundation. The atomic data must appear there. For example, the organization needs to store the details of each sale separately. If sales are accumulated by month, there is no way to do a daily analysis against the month's sales.

The level of granularity of data makes a big difference for analytics. The foundation of data may contain summarized or otherwise derived data. The foundation of data must contain the atomic data that supports summarization or derivation.

If summarized data is placed in the foundation, storing the algorithms used to create the summarization is necessary. The analyst using the data needs to know how the summarizations were created.

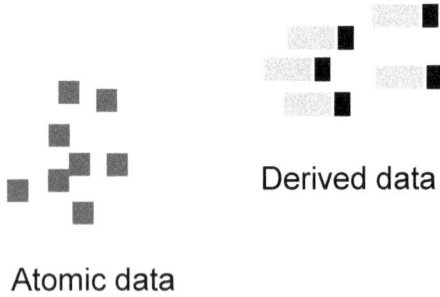

Derived data

Atomic data

Figure 4: Data resides at the atomic level and, if necessary, at a summary level.

Integrity of naming conventions

In addition to the value of data represented by the name of the data, the integrity of the naming conventions that were used to name the data is also important. In particular:

- No two different units of data should have the same name
- No two names should refer to the same unit of data.

For example, there are two databases named REVENUE. The databases are quite different. One database is for products sold in Kansas and the other database is the data that represents sales made across the US in 2017. In this case, two units of data are named the same but represent very different things.

Integration of data

Finally, data in the solid foundation of data MUST be integrated. Of all of the factors to consider in building a solid foundation of data, this is the most difficult one. As an example of the need for integration of data before it enters the foundation, consider three pieces of data:

- Revenue - $3,000
- Revenue - $5,000
- Revenue - $9,000.

It appears that this data is acceptable because all three elements of data represent revenue. However, one type of revenue is from Australia. Another type of revenue is from Canada. The third type of revenue is from the US. You cannot meaningfully add or combine the data together until you adjust the data for the country of origin. The need for data integration extends far beyond considering the country of origin, yet that is necessary to establish a robust data foundation. There are many, many more cases of the need for integration.

The solid foundation of data needed to support new technologies must be integrated.

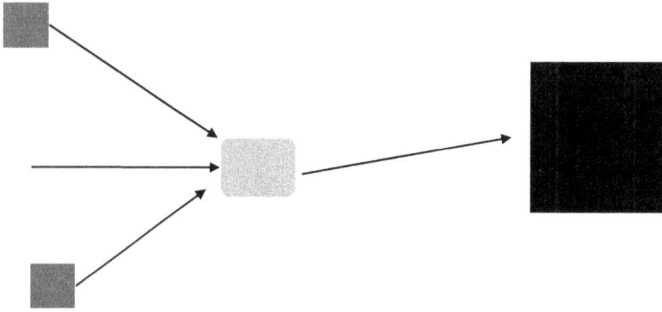

Figure 5: Data must be integrated in the foundation.

Summary

To use new technologies successfully, there must be a firm foundation of data on which to use technology. Unfortunately, most corporations do not have that foundation. Furthermore, most corporations are unwilling to put in the hard work required to rebuild the foundation.

Although AI can help, calculations, summarizations, and basic answers produced by generative AI tools from structured data can be wrong. The problems occur when end users trust these outputs.

Also, improvements can be made to the foundation of data over time. However, if the improvement of the existing foundation of data is done over time, the users of the new technology need to be made aware of the limitations of the data on which they operate their new technologies.

Garbage in, garbage out (GIGO)!

Chapter 2

Business Value and Foundation Data

To achieve an objective, data collections need to be focused on areas like:

- Medical research, designed to improve the health of human beings

- Science, designed to learn more about some aspect of science

- Government, designed to learn more about the constituents and activities of the constituents of the government

- Business, designed to learn more about customers, products, sales, and other things important to the conduct of business.

This chapter focuses on enhancing the health of businesses. The proper setup of your foundation of data, which drives better decision making and new technology, ultimately leads to higher profitability. Each collection of data must have a purpose before being collected or set up. These purposes set the direction for collecting data. As such, the direction of the collection of data found in the foundation of data for a business sets up the pathway to greater profitability.

The focus of the foundation

When data is not focused, the data becomes difficult and confusing to use. The data is unorganized. Data relationships become very disorderly. In one minute, the organization analyzes one thing. The next minute, the organization looks at something entirely unrelated.

Given that much analysis is done in a heuristic manner, most organizations need as much help as possible to remain focused. As an example of unfocused data, consider a single collection of data that contains:

- Police conviction records
- The annual GNP of Chile
- The medical records of St Luke's Hospital
- The specifications for the production of an airplane.

The data is so scattered and unrelatable that it is doubtful that anything useful will ever come out of it.

The more focused the data in the foundation, the better the chance of success.

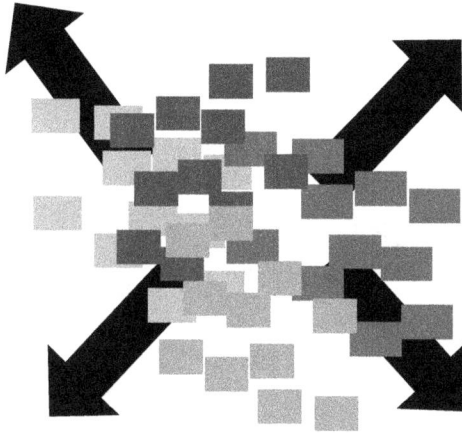

Figure 6: Data that is not focused usually leads nowhere.

Organizing the foundation

Not only does the data in the foundation need to be focused, the data in the foundation also needs to be organized. The organization of data in the foundation permits:

- Finding the data
- Relating the data together
- Managing the volume of collected data.

Of these reasons, the need to relate data together is usually first on the list for the analyst. Data is typically related together using the conventional key/foreign key relationship. The ability to relate data together greatly enhances the range of questions that the analyst can ask.

Consider the following simple diagram as an example of how business data can be organized into a solid foundation.

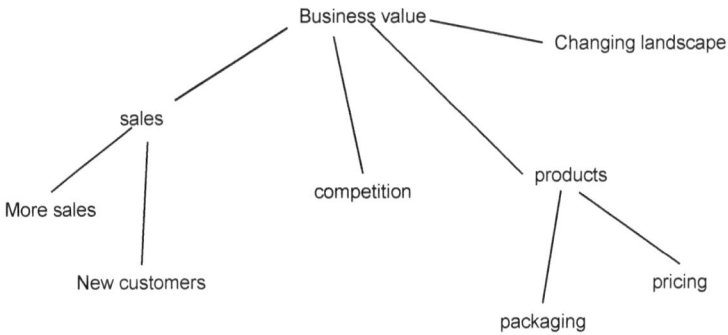

Figure 7: There are many facets to business value.

The diagram (which is hardly complete) shows several different things:

- There are many facets to the conduct of business
- Most of the aspects of business can be arranged in a hierarchical fashion
- Some of the aspects are related and some are not.

For example, when examining profitability, one of the most important aspects of profitability is the sales that have occurred and the total cost of those sales. Once sales are discussed, the next important aspect is how to increase sales without incurring excessive costs. In the same vein, how to engage more customers becomes a topic of analysis.

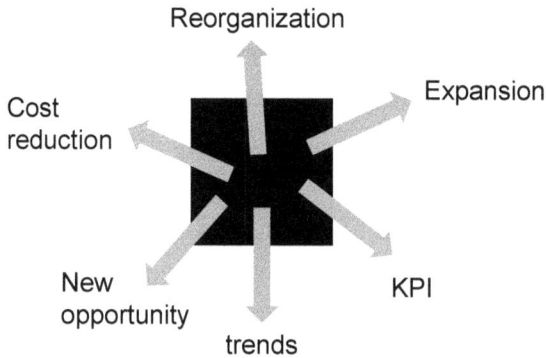

Figure 8: Business value can be driven from the foundation of data.

Analysis

Once the data foundation has been focused and structured properly, the possibilities for business analysis are in place. The business can answer such questions as:

- Is pricing optimal?
- Are we losing or gaining customers?
- Can we package our product differently?
- Is competition starting to eat into our revenue?
- What new products can be introduced?
- Should we expand into a new geographical territory?

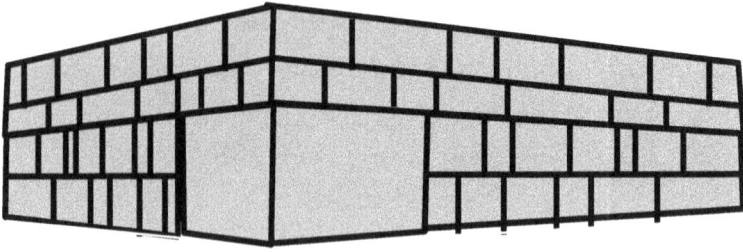

Figure 9: A solid foundation of data sets the stage for prosperity.

Summary

The foundation that supports business requires a solid foundation of data. The foundation needs to be focused and internally organized. Once built properly, the solid data foundation can support new technologies and growth.

Chapter 3

The Origins of Foundation Data

Most organizations have a foundation of data on which to process new technology. Where did that foundation come from? What were its origins?

Legacy data

Most organizations' data foundations have come from years of collecting what is termed "legacy data."

The term "legacy data" refers to the data generated as a byproduct of processing earlier applications. So, what are the origins of legacy data? Where did it come from and what are its characteristics?

Early computation

In the very beginning, when computers first appeared on the horizon, the corporation became enamored of the idea of computerizing its business. The corporation was correct in its assumption that the computer could provide a great advantage for the corporation. Unfortunately, the corporation lacked experience in building and deploying the necessary applications.

One day, the corporation selected a vendor, typically a hardware vendor. The vendor introduced its technology. With that technology, the corporation began designing and developing the applications it needed.

How we got here

In the earliest days, there were no software packages to purchase and no consultants to hire for building the early applications.

All organizations started with a single application that began to throw off data due to processing. Sometimes, the data was merely discarded. Most often, the data was collected and stored in some form. In short order, the volumes of data thrown off by the application began to collect and multiply. On the first day, a small amount of data was collected. By year's end, even more data had been collected.

The organization hardly stopped at the building of one application. Some of the applications were built on technology from the first vendor. Some of the newer applications were from a different vendor. As these applications were built and put into operation, they began to generate even more data.

At the time, no one noticed that the data being thrown off was entirely distinct, unique, and incompatible with the other sorts of data created by other applications. Soon, a trickle of stored data turned into a significant torrent.

Heavily contributing to the disparity of data being thrown off by the many applications was the fact that the development of data was designed to fit the needs of exactly one set of users. The user was interviewed, and the development manager specifically catered to the application's design to meet the user's specific needs and requirements. This process is called the Traditional Software Development Lifecycle or SDLC. The common term for developing these systems is "The Waterfall Method." There are several problems with adhering to the SDLC due to its strict nature, but one major issue is that its narrow focus often overlooks the data requirements and data storage needs of users outside the initial scope of the application. At the time, this was the accepted practice of system design. Developers were taught to build and optimize the application around the needs of the ultimate user.

The net result of this approach to the building of applications was that each design and application was focused on the needs of a different user. In other words, the applications had no consideration or even thought about the need to conform to a standard of data across the organization. What was being produced was application-based data, not data for the corporation. Some of the many aspects of design that were unique to the application included topics from the last chapter, such as:

- **Definition of data**. Product meant one thing in one application and something different in another application.

- **Naming of data**. Revenue was REV in one application and XW-76-P in another application.

- **Data calculated differently in each application**. Interest was calculated at 5% in one application and 6% in another application.

- **Data encoded differently in each application**. One application encoded gender as M/F, and another application encoded gender as MALE/FEMALE.

- **Physical description of the data**. In one place customer was defined to be Pic x(35). In another place, customer was varchar(50).

Each group of end users of the application was satisfied with their own application, but the needs of users outside of each functional area of the company were not taken into account. The needs of the company were not taken

into account. The ability to integrate data with other data
sources was not taken into account.

The disparity of design consistency was especially true for transaction processing applications, such as airline reservation processing, bank teller processing, and manufacturing control systems.

Transaction processing systems were important because there was a wide interest in the data generated by the transaction processing application. Originally, the transaction processing system was designed to meet the needs of a single user. Once the transaction data was processed, the data that was thrown off was interesting and useful to many other functional areas within the organization.

The net result of different applications producing lots of uncoordinated and distinctly non-standardized data was that a pile of tangled data was produced. There was a lot of data that could not be easily integrated. The pile of data represented a lot of disparate applications, and there was no corporate understanding of the data.

The integration of data found in the pile was important because accounting/sales/marketing wanted to use the data for their purposes. Those organizations wanted to look across the entire organization, not at a single application.

As a simple example of the conflict that arose, consider that Application ABC was written to satisfy the needs of the store vendors making point-to-point sales in a store, where the sales clerk meets face-to-face with the customer. Meanwhile, Application BCD was written to manage sales from the Internet. Orders were collected from the Internet and then processed.

Each application had its own interpretation of what a sale was. The definitions across different departments did not align. When accounting used the pile of transaction data, accounting had to add fundamentally different data together. It was like adding apples and oranges together. Both are fruit. Nevertheless, apples are fundamentally different from oranges.

Figure 10: The net result was a tangle of data due to the execution of many uncoordinated applications.

To make matters even more confusing, some applications were built using the technology from one vendor, and others were built using the technology from another vendor. The net result was that there were significant difficulties in trying to extract corporate information from the vast amount of data generated by the various applications.

Furthermore, as time went on, there was even more data. There was a greater demand for corporate data. The disparity between the different types of data continued to grow each day.

Summary

What, then, were the results of the jumble of data collected from the processing occurring in the organization? The results showed that different departments were making very different decisions. Department A analyzed the data and stated that the corporation was losing market share. The recommended posture was to maximize revenue from the existing customer base and become as profitable as the organization could become.

A second department analyzed the same data and decided that the company was increasing its market share and that now was the time to spend more and try to gain even more market share.

A third department decided that the company was stable and that spending money was a waste of time for gaining market share and, at the same time, not maximizing the revenue stream.

No corporation can live with different parts going in individual directions. It is like a symphony orchestra where the violins are playing music from Mozart, the horns are playing *God Bless America*, and the piano is playing the Beatles' *Yesterday*. The result was not music at all, despite the skills of the orchestra ensemble. To be successful, the various departments of the company must work in unison with one another.

This entire dilemma started because of the unintegrated jumble of data that was being thrown off by the applications.

In the final analysis, the application data being thrown off was simply unacceptable to serve the needs of the corporation.

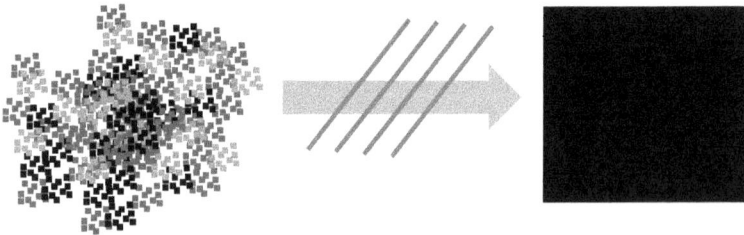

Figure 11: The motley collection of legacy data does not make a proper basis for a solid foundation of data.

Chapter 4

From Legacy to Foundation

Most organizations built applications and let the data accumulate over the years. This collection of data is normally called "legacy data." Most organizations believe that this diverse collection of data is a suitable foundation for analytical processing and can be leveraged to utilize new technology. The old legacy data is fraught with inconsistent and incomplete data, and data that simply cannot be used as a basis for analytical processing. Legacy data is not fit to form the foundation of data to perform analytical processing or processing conducted by new technologies.

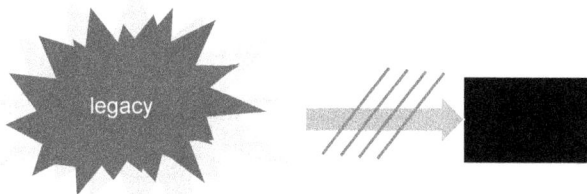

Figure 12: Legacy data simply is not a good way to build the platform that is needed for the foundation of data.

35

Structured data

Legacy data was thrown from the applications in a form called structured data. To create structured data, a transaction typically occurs within the business that generates the data. This data is usually a reflection of the business that has transpired.

Data is called structured because the physical makeup and storage of each respective data element in the database is the same. Of course, the contents of the records differ, but their structure is identical. For example, I went to the grocery store and bought some milk. A transaction based on the sale showing that milk was sold on a given day at a given price. A record of data is created as a result of the purchase. The next person in line buys some bread. A separate record shows that bread was sold on a given day at a price. The structure of the record of the bread sale and the structure of the record of the sale of milk made by the person next in line are identical. The contents of the records are very different.

In an earlier time, there was only structured data. It is structured data that makes up the vast majority of the content of the legacy environment.

The data architect

Then, a new kind of professional appeared in the organization: the data architect. The data architect knew about the details of database design, data administration, and programming. The data architect could also look into the future and see the larger picture of the needs of the corporation.

To use an analogy, you want to build a bridge. Certainly, you need carpenters and cement workers. You also need someone to think about:

- What kind of traffic is the bridge going to need to hold?

- What kind of atmospheric conditions will the bridge be subjected to?

- How can the bridge be repaired over time?

It is not carpenters and cement workers who will answer these larger questions. It is an architect.

Just like the construction of a bridge, the development of a data architecture requires the attention and skills of both detail-oriented workers and those responsible for addressing the long-term issues related to the data architecture.

In an earlier day, when the first applications were being built, there was no need for an architect. All that was needed was an application designer and developer.

When it comes to building a foundation of accessible, complete, accurate, and relatable data, there is definitely a need for a data architect.

Transforming legacy data

As data passes into the foundation from the legacy environment, the data goes through a fundamental transformation. Application data turns into corporate data. To envision such a transformation, consider the following diagram.

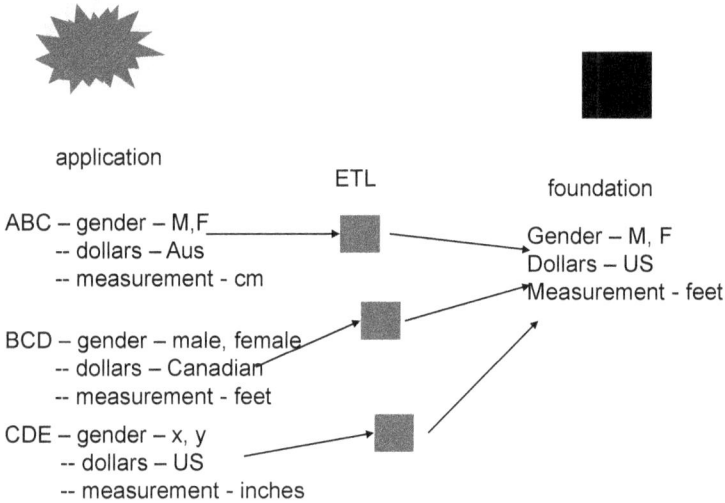

application

ETL

foundation

ABC – gender – M,F
-- dollars – Aus
-- measurement - cm

Gender – M, F
Dollars – US
Measurement - feet

BCD – gender – male, female
-- dollars – Canadian
-- measurement - feet

CDE – gender – x, y
-- dollars – US
-- measurement - inches

Figure 13: Data transformation.

There are three applications. Each application designer has chosen their own way to represent data. The first application represents gender as M/F. The next application represents gender as male/female. The third application represents gender as X/Y.

There are other differences as well. Each application has a dollar amount represented. However, one dollar amount is in Australian dollars. Another is Canadian dollars. The third is US dollars.

There is a field of data that is measured in centimeters, feet, and inches. While each application certainly has the right to organize data as it sees fit, when it comes to looking across the entire organization, the disparity in how data is organized prevents the organization from having a true enterprise view.

What is needed is a basic transformation of data to achieve an analysis of data across the corporation. The transformation from legacy to foundation is typically accomplished through a technology called ETL (extract, transform, and load). The data from the legacy application passes through ETL and emerges as singularly defined data. Now, the corporation can use the data for analysis across the enterprise.

The data model

So, how is the transformation process from legacy to foundation accomplished? The answer is that the transformation process is guided by means of a data model. The data model sits above the foundation and depicts the future state of the data.

In many cases, the data model depicts current data. The data model also serves as a guide for future data transformations. As such, the data model is useful for both current and future transformations.

The data model is an essential tool of data architecture. The data model reflects the state of corporate data. As such, the data model becomes the guide for building the foundation data. Stated differently, the data model shapes the foundation.

The data model is often complex. In addition, the data model is often quite large. Because of the size and complexity of the data model, the data model is often constructed in three ways: at a high level, mid-level, and low level.

These three ways of depicting the data model are analogous to the world, the state of Texas, and a roadmap of Dallas, Texas. The globe depicts the locations of countries and continents. The state of Texas includes Dallas, Houston, and El Paso. The map of Dallas shows the route from the Cowboys' football stadium to downtown Dallas.

You would not use the map of Dallas to find your way to New York City. Conversely, you would not use the map of the globe to find your way from the Eiffel Tower to the Louvre. The data model works in the same fashion.

The sections of the data model are:

- High level: the ERD (entity relationship diagram)
- Mid-level: the DIS (data item set)
- Low level: DDL (data definition language).

The ERD depicts the major categories of data and the relationships between those categories. The DIS provides details about each entity. The DDL represents the way the data will be defined in the system.

There is one DIS for every major category defined in the ERD.

The ERD contains:

- The major categories of information
- The relationship between those categories.

For example, an ERD may contain products, orders, and shipments.

The DIS contains such things as:

- Keys
- Attributes
- Relationship information.

For example, the DIS may look like:

- Customer
- Account number
- Customer name
- Customer address
- Customer gender
- Customer telephone number.

The DDL is the precise definition of data that will be used to generate the description of the data for the system. The DDL might look like:

- Record_id varchar(50)
- Customer_acct char(12) key
- Customer_name varchar(35)
- Customer_address varchar(60)
- Customer_gender binary
- Customer_telephone numeric(10).

The relationships between the different levels of the model are:

- Each major subject area has its own DIS
- Each DIS has one or more DDLs that describe the data inside the DIS.

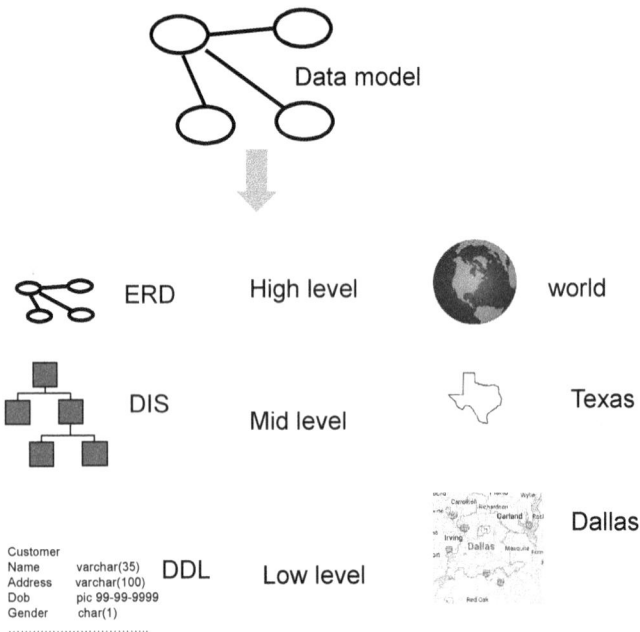

Figure 14: The structure of the data model.

When is the data model complete?

The answer is never! The data model remains in constant motion as long as the business continues to evolve. The data model reflects the business of the corporation. The corporate business model changes all the time. Many factors determine the changes to the data model, including:

- Legislative changes
- Economic conditions
- Competition
- New opportunities
- Mergers.

The data model is finished when the company ceases to exist.

Initially, the data model requires a significant design effort. As the changes occur over time, the alterations to the data model are very small and incremental.

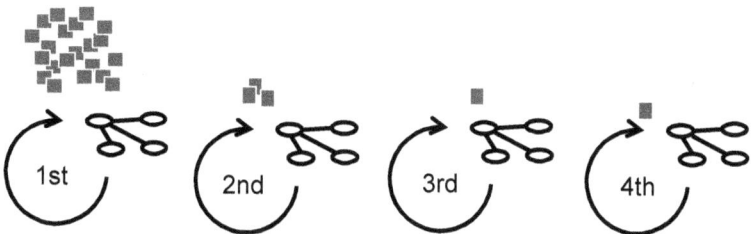

Figure 15: The first iteration of the development of the data model is fairly large; each iteration thereafter is usually just a tweak.

When shaping the foundation data, the data model becomes the blueprint.

The data model is used by a variety of roles including:

- Programmer
- End user analyst
- Designer
- Manager.

While the data model is most useful at the start of the construction of the foundation, it is also useful for many years, as new systems are built, business conditions change, and technology changes.

Kinds of data

The issue is that the transformation of application data to a foundation only applies to structured data. In fact, there is much more data that exists other than structured data, including:

- Email
- Internet
- Contracts
- Telephone conversations
- Call centers.

Text is woven into the fabric of doing business. There is much more text in the corporation than there is structured data.

> *A great amount of important information is wrapped up in text.*

Another type of data found in the corporation is analog data. Analog data is data created by machines in operation. There are a wide variety of machines that generate data, including:

- Watches
- Lathes
- Cars
- Railroads
- Drones.

A challenge is bringing all three types of data into the foundation.

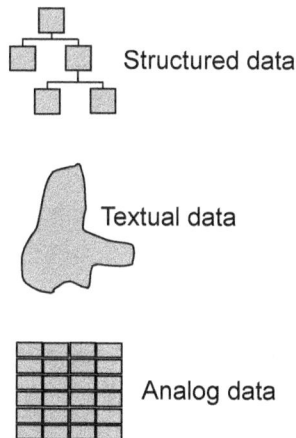

Figure 16: Soon other forms of data began to enter the corporation.

These different forms of data have very different characteristics. Yet they all contribute to the foundation of data that is needed to service new technologies.

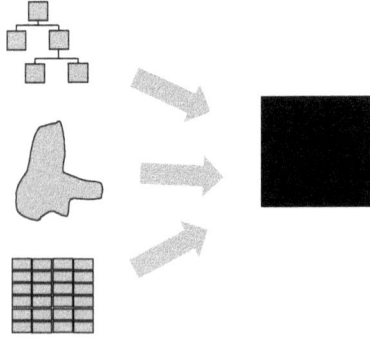

Figure 17: It was recognized that there was a need to bring the other forms of data into the foundation of data.

Summary

Legacy data does not provide a proper foundation for data. Legacy data is application-oriented and does not reflect corporate data. To achieve corporate data, a transformation of data must be done. The transformation of legacy data is achieved by building a data model and using the model to guide the transformation process. The data model reflects the current and future needs of data at the corporate level. The data model has three levels:

- High level: ERD
- Mid-level: DIS
- Low level: DDL.

While the transformation of legacy data to corporate data is a good start to building the foundation, textual and analog data need to be included as well.

Chapter 5

The Data Architect

The primary goal of the data architect was to oversee the development and implementation of the data foundation and its accompanying data model. Soon, the data architect role expanded to other areas within the corporation. The data architect has both a business and technical background.

The architect has the final say when asked, "How do I make changes to the data model and/or the data in the foundation?" No one besides the data architect was allowed to go into the data model or the foundation of data and make changes.

The primary responsibilities of the data architect is to oversee the input into the foundation and the data model, as well as to manage the usage of the foundation and the data model (the information flowing out). Additionally, the data architect occasionally makes changes to the foundation and/or model.

The activities of the data architect

The data architect has a very diverse job. One day, the data architect is busy addressing a technical problem, and the next day, the data architect works with users on a business problem. A wide variety of tasks and skills are involved in being a data architect.

The data architect needs to be involved in the development process. The data architect advises on such subjects as:

- Corporate conventions
- If the data already exists somewhere else
- The best way to structure the data for development
- What encoding is already being used
- What key structures already exist and their definition
- Volume of data and how best to handle it.

The data architect is also involved in selecting software and technology. The data architect is involved in discussions of:

- How will the new technology best fit with existing technology?
- Is the new technology going to overlap with existing technology?
- What business value does the new technology bring?

Transformation is one of the most important areas in which the data architect is involved. Transformation includes structured data, textual data, and analog data. Some of the discussions the data architect is involved in include:

- What transformation logic is involved?
- How much data is involved?
- How will the transformed data mesh with existing data?
- How will the transformation logic be tested?
- How often will transformation be done?

The data architect is also interested in installation. Some of the concerns of the data architect include:

- Who will do the installation?
- How long will it take?
- How complex is the installation?

The data architect also maintains the transformation process and implements it in the foundation. The transformation process constantly changes as the business and foundation data change. Some of the considerations the data architect has with the ongoing maintenance of the transformation process include:

- Who is making the changes?
- Will the changes impact existing data?
- Will the changes affect the analysis previously done on the foundation of data?
- Will the changes impact or hamstring the current analysis being done?
- How many resources will the changes require and how long will it take to make the changes?

- Are there any maintenance changes that need to be done but have not been done?

The data architect career path

The starting point can be programming. Whether an architect has done extensive programming or not, the architect needs to know how to program and its associated pitfalls. The data architect needs to be able to estimate the duration of projects and identify their key milestones. A data architect who needs to understand programming is like a construction architect who needs to understand how to drive nails or lay concrete. The construction architect doesn't actually have to drive nails or lay concrete, but they need to understand the process of driving nails or laying concrete. Similarly, the data architect needs to have a grounding in programming. Then, one day, the data architect becomes a designer. Designing is similar to programming. The data architect needs to understand what happens when designing programs and systems. The data architect needs to be aware of the pitfalls and know how to estimate the project accurately.

After the design process, the data architect needs to understand the database. The data architect needs to have a solid understanding of the processes involved in creating a database. As in previous cases, the data architect needs to understand the mistakes made in designing and building a database. Certainly, the data architect needs to understand database management systems (DBMS).

The next skill the data architect needs to acquire is that of being an analyst, of using the system to solve a business problem. The activity of being an analyst exposes the data architect to two important things:

- The usability of the system that has been created
- The relationship of the system to business value.

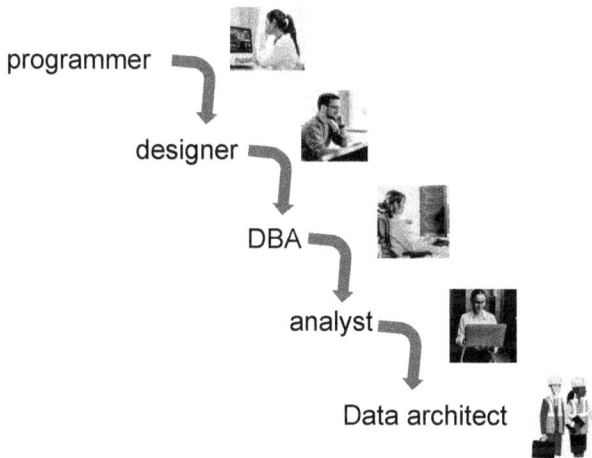

programmer

designer

DBA

analyst

Data architect

Figure 18: The typical career path of the data architect.

The data architect must have a desire to deliver business value. Without an appreciation for delivering business value, the data architect may become an entirely competent technician disconnected from his/her company. That is a formula for disaster. Finally, after acquiring all these skills, the data architect is prepared to face the numerous challenges of constructing and managing the corporation's data.

If any of these steps are missed, the data architect will inevitably have a blind spot. Unfortunately, that blind spot will lead to unfortunate and negative consequences.

Perspectives

The perspective of the data architect is one that encompasses both long-term and short-term perspectives simultaneously.

The long-term perspective of the data architect includes such topics as:

- **Strategic direction**. The data architect must ensure that the foundation of data being laid will support the organization's long-term business needs.

- **Revenue/profit**. The data architect must ensure that the foundation of data supports the organization's revenue generation and profitability.

- **Analytical relevance**. The data architect must ensure that the data being collected and organized in the foundation and the data model is relevant to the analytical needs of the organization.

The short-term perspective of the data architect includes such topics as:

- **Accessibility to the foundation of data**. Accessibility refers to both the electronic accessibility of the foundation and the descriptive information necessary to locate data within the foundation.

- **Accuracy of the foundation**. The data architect needs to ensure that the data existing in the foundation is indeed accurate. If inaccurate data is discovered, the data architect must tend to the repair of the foundation.

- **Completeness**. Not only does the data architect have to worry about the accuracy of the data in the foundation, but the data architect also has to take into account the completeness of the data and the currency of the data.

The issues discussed here are just the SHORT list of the things the data architect needs to consider. In fact, there is an even longer list.

Indirectly, the data architect affects almost everyone in the corporation: salespeople, engineers, finance, inventory management, and marketing.

Summary

While organizations need a foundation and a data model, they also require someone to build and manage these foundations and data models. The organization is responsible for the foundation and the data architect is responsible for the data model.

The data architect has to have a working knowledge of a variety of skills:

- Technical skills
- Organizational skills
- Business skills.

The data architect needs to have both long-term and short-term perspectives.

Chapter 6

Transformation and Data Architecture

A subject that consultants and vendors often avoid discussing is the transformation of data. Vendors and consultants prefer everything to be nice, neat, and orderly. The transformation of data is definitely not nice, neat, and orderly.

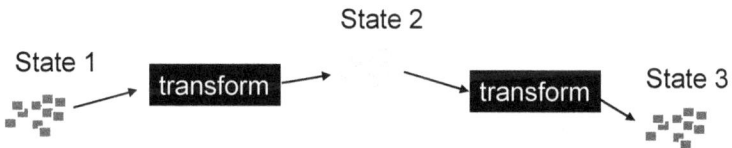

Figure 19: Data is constantly being transformed.

There are actually many forms of data transformation. Data can be transformed in one way, two ways, and many ways, and all at the same time.

Why do transformations?

Transformation of data is performed to make the data useful for the person conducting the analysis.

Using an analogy, suppose a person asks for a wine glass. The person expects to receive a clean, clear glass suitable for holding wine. In fact, the wine glass is just a product of the refinement of sand. When a person asks for a wine glass, you could hand them a handful of sand and tell them to use it to make their own glass. Which, in theory, they could do. However, the expectation is that you get something useful when you ask for something.

When someone requests data, they expect it to be presented in a form that is both useful and meaningful to them.

Simple transformation

Perhaps the simplest form of data transformation is the simple summarization of data. The data appears initially as a single occurrence. Then, someone needs to see that single occurrence of data summarized (or otherwise calculated) with some other data.

Summarizing and performing simple data calculations are basic forms of data transformation.

Deselection is also a simple form of transformation of data. Suppose there are three records of data: one from January, one from April, and one from July. For whatever reason, the person analyzing the data does not want the record from January. So, the record from January does not move along with the other records that are not from January as the data is transformed.

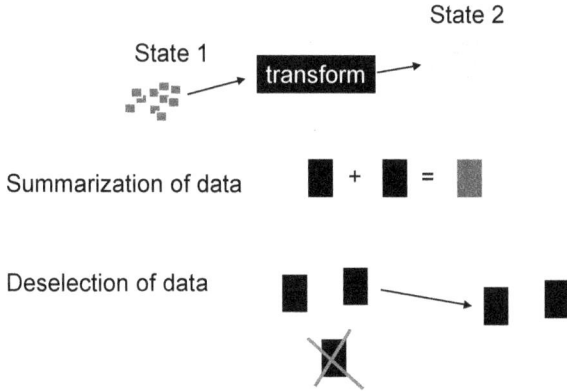

Figure 20: Summarizing and deselecting data.

Recalculating data is another form of transformation. Suppose there are records of revenue for the US, Australia, and Canada. Before the records can be meaningfully combined, they must be in a common currency.

Another form of data transformation is the reorganization of data. Reorganization refers to the merging of records and/or the manipulation of the data structure. Suppose there is an annual statement of some activity relating to an account. In another place, there is a month-by-month accounting of activity against the same account. The user would like to see the monthly statements merged with the annual statement.

Another example of data transformation occurs when a daily record is created for an activity. The end user doesn't want to see the daily activity. Instead, the end user would like to see a synopsis of the daily activity on a month-by-month and yearly basis. This type of data transformation may involve numerous activities. Summarization may be used. Restructuring data may be necessary. Separating normal data from outlier data may be required. Amalgamating data may be required. This form of transformation may become quite complex.

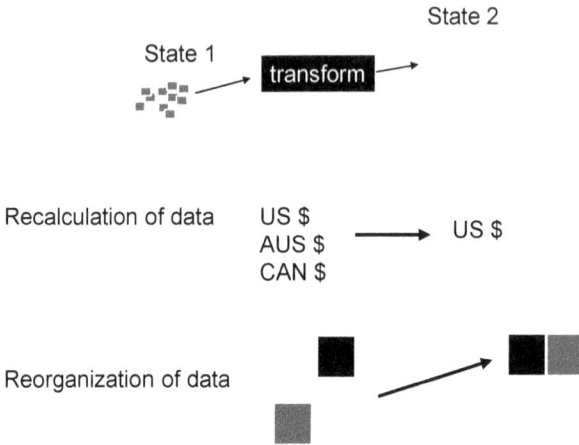

Figure 21: Recalculating and reorganizing data.

Another form of data transformation is the transformation required to consolidate encoded values. Suppose there are three files. In one file, gender is represented by the letters M or F. In another file, the gender is male or female. In yet another file, gender is 1 or 0. To make the files intelligible and usable for the analyst, the gender must be translated into a single value.

Another form of transformation of data exists when an object is being measured, but the unit of measurement is different. Suppose the object is measured in centimeters in one file. In another file, the object is measured in inches. In yet another file, the object is measured in feet. When the data is transformed, the object is measured in a single unit of measurement.

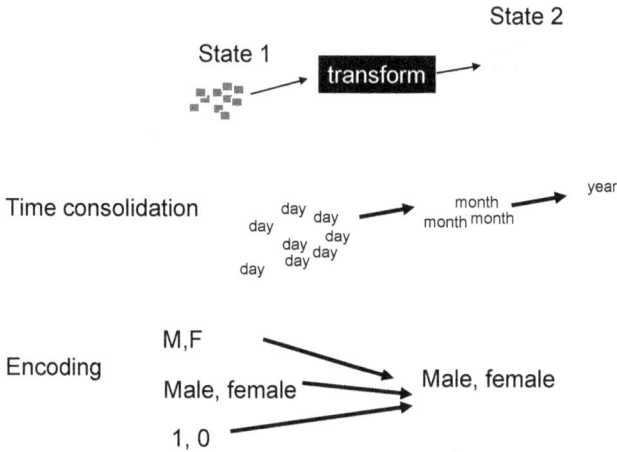

Figure 22: Consolidating and encoding data.

Another form of transformation in textual processing is a mixture of languages. In one file, the language used is Spanish. In the second file, the language is English. In the third file, the language is Portuguese. To process the file successfully, the languages need to be translated into a common language.

The transformations of data described here merely scratch the surface of what transformation of data means. It should be noted that multiple types of data transformations can occur simultaneously against the same data.

Transformation of data is a complex yet necessary reality.

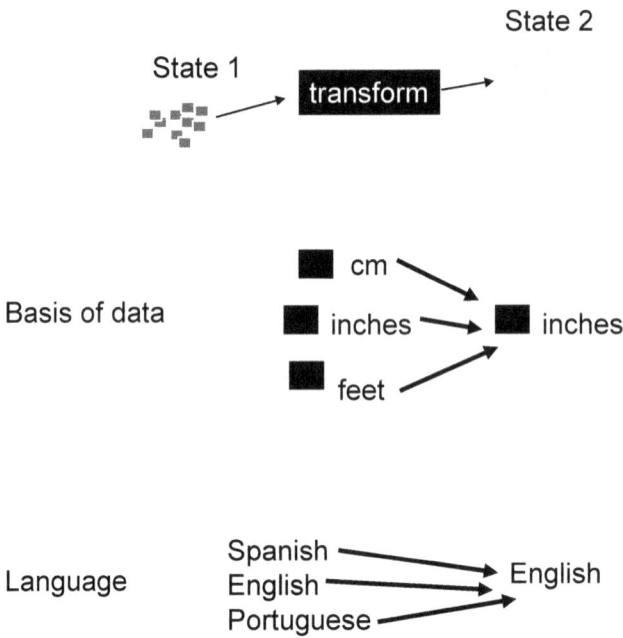

State 2

State 1

transform

Basis of data

- cm
- inches → inches
- feet

Language

Spanish
English → English
Portuguese

Figure 23: Basis of data and language.

Who needs data transformation?

So, who needs to have data transformed? The answer is that nearly everyone needs transformations of data.

To understand the need for data transformation, suppose a clerk at a store makes a sale. The sale is rung up at the register. It seems simple enough. However, many people require a record of the sale.

Accountants need to know about the transaction to prepare revenue and tax statements, including such things as:

- The date of the transaction
- The amount of the transaction
- Were local taxes paid
- The location of the transaction.

Marketing also needs to be aware of the transaction, including:

- Was the object purchased on sale?
- Where was the object purchased?
- At what time of day and what day of the week was the object purchased?
- Was the object purchased in conjunction with another object?
- Were discount coupons used in the purchase?

Management needs its own information about the purchase, including:

- How many other objects of the same kind were purchased in the same store? In the same month? In the same department?
- How long has the object sat on the shelf before being purchased?
- Which shelf was the object on?

Finance needs to know:

- Was the object on consignment?
- What kind of third-party display of the object was used, if any?

In short, a diversity of organizations has an interest in different aspects of the purchase that has been made. The record of the purchase needs to be able to accommodate all these needs, and it must be transformed to meet the audience's needs using the data.

It is seen that each of the different groups of people interested in the purchase has their own informational needs.

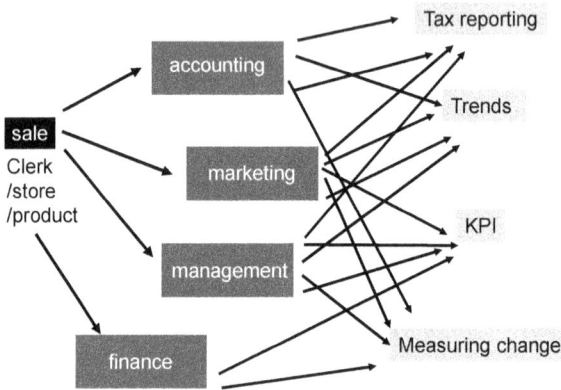

Figure 24: Each of the different organizations has its own use for the transformed data.

Business value

When considering the transformation of data, one of the most important factors to consider is the distinct business value that different types of data bring. Nearly, but not all, structured data has business value. Some of the textual data have business value and some do not. Very little of the analog data has business value.

To understand this phenomenon, consider the emails an organization receives. Throughout the day, numerous emails are processed through the system. Some are emails telling jokes. Some emails talk about the fortunes of the local football team. Additionally, some emails concern business transactions. Depending on the organization and its business, perhaps 40% to 50% of the emails are business-related.

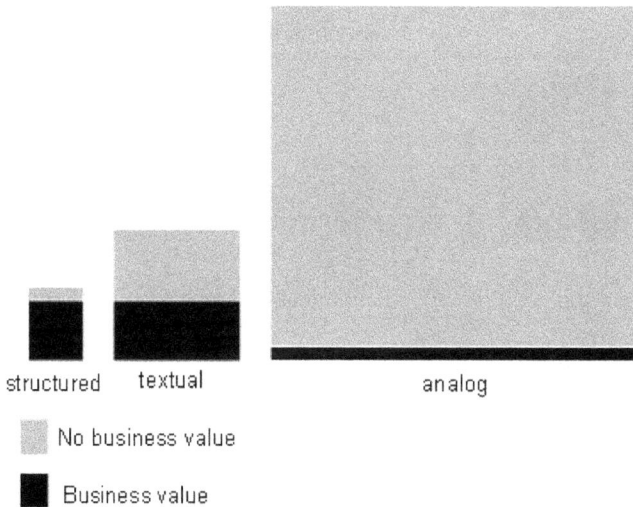

Figure 25: There is a very different ratio of business value to no business value across the different kinds of data.

Now consider analog data. Analog data is data that is generated by a machine. Suppose there is an analog measurement of output produced by a lathe in a factory. The lathe sits there all day, producing output as it works. The data that measures the output merely registers one product after another as it is run into the factory. Then, at 1:23 am, there is an interruption in power at the manufacturing plant. Because of the power interruption, the lathe produces a faulty part. The system takes note of the malfunction. When examining the register of the output, 99.99% of the data is normal, but 0.01% is defective. Only a tiny percentage of the analog data is of interest. The small percentage that is of interest is of high interest, because the manufacturer does not want to send a defective part to the public.

A small percentage of analog data is of great concern to the company.

Technology for transformation

Due to the differences in business value ratios among various types of data and other factors, the technology required to transform data varies significantly.

Structured data uses ETL technology. Textual data used textual ETL. In addition, analog data requires a distillation process. The different types of technology that are required is shown in the following diagram.

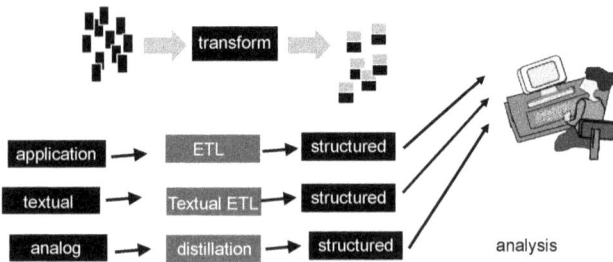

Figure 26: Each form of data has its own method of doing the transformation.

Analytics across the different types of data

An interesting question is, "Why does data have to be structured to be analyzed?" The answer is that data does not have to be structured to be analyzed. As long as there is only a very small amount of data to be analyzed, it can be analyzed manually, in a free-form manner. If there is more than a handful of data, then the data needs to be structured and analyzed. That is because the technology that does analysis requires that the data be structured. If it were possible to perform analytics on large amounts of unstructured data, then there would be no need to structure the data before analysis.

Another interesting question is, "In doing analysis, is it possible to mix the different types of data together even when the different kinds of data are structured?"

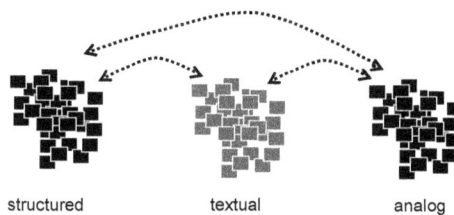

structured   textual   analog

Figure 27: Can analytics be done across the different kinds of data?

The answer is that some different types of data can be mixed, and mixing other types of data in an analysis is difficult. For example, structured data and textual data can usually be freely mixed. That is because textual data often uses the language and terms that are found in structured data. On the other hand, it is not often that analog data and textual data can be mixed. There usually is not much overlap between the two kinds of data. The same considerations apply to structured data and analog data. There just is not much overlap between the two types of data. Then there is the question, "Can all three of the types of data be mixed in a single analysis?"

The answer is that this type of analysis can only be possible very, very rarely. The only circumstance where it is possible to analyze all three types of data is where a common key exists across all three environments. While there may be a common key, the circumstances are rare.

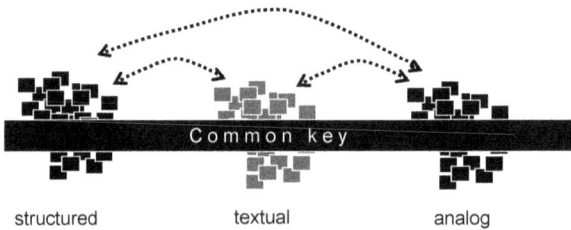

Figure 28: The only way data can be compared across the different kinds of data is if there happens to be a common key across the spectrum.

Summary

Transformation of data is an everyday occurrence. Data needs to be transformed because different organizations have different needs for the same data. Transformation occurs with different technologies. One of the contributing reasons why different technologies undergo transformation is due to the varying ratios of business relevance to different types of data.

Chapter 7

Evolution of Database Design and Probability of Access

One of the essential aspects of data architecture is a database and database design. In many ways, database design is like the plumbing of a house—an absolute necessity to living in the house and being comfortable but unintelligible to the occupants of the house.

Over the years, database design has evolved. What started as a very simple discipline is now a much more complex discipline.

Figure 29: The evolution of database and database design.

Storage media

One way to approach the subject of the evolution of database design is by the media on which data has been stored. The media that stores databases has a profound effect on the way databases are designed.

At a very high level, the first media on which databases were stored was on punched cards, often called Hollerith cards. Punched cards were only used for a short time in the early days of computation. While punched cards were a starting point, there were lots of problems with punched cards. Punched cards were:

- Cumbersome to deal with
- Limited to 80 columns of data per card
- Could only handle a small amount of data
- Expensive
- Wasteful of precious natural resources
- Can only be read sequentially
- Easy to drop.

Then, after punched cards, data was housed on magnetic tape files. Sometimes, the data on magnetic tape files was called "master files." Magnetic tape files were once widely used. In fact, in some places, they are still used today, although not as widely as they once were or in the same manner as they were previously.

A magnetic tape file is a long ribbon coated with oxide. The electronic information is electronically written on the oxide on the ribbon.

The advantages of magnetic tape files over punched cards are that much more data could be stored on a magnetic tape file than on punched cards, and the record size on magnetic tape was not limited to 80 bytes.

There were some major drawbacks to the magnetic tape file. The biggest drawback to a magnetic tape file was that to find a single record, you had to search the entire file. It took quite a while to search an entire magnetic tape file. Another significant drawback was the fact that the oxide stripped off the file easily, making the file worthless once the oxide was gone.

After magnetic tape files came disc storage. Disc storage in its many forms is widely used today. Disc storage is a device that is constantly spinning. The read and write heads of the disc device operate on fixed electronic media, storing and accessing data.

Disc devices were fast. In addition, with disc storage, you can access a record of data directly. You did not have to spin through the whole file to find a single record. In the very early days, disc storage was expensive. Then disc storage began to be widely produced, and the storage cost dropped dramatically.

OLTP

Once disc storage became widely used and inexpensive, disc technology was used to support online transaction processing (OLTP). Online transaction processing became very popular, enabling the development of new applications that were previously impossible to create. In many ways, online transaction processing brought the computer directly into the heart of the business. Applications such as airline reservations and bank teller processing became possible. With online processing, the computer transitioned from being a useful tool to being at the heart of the business. Transaction processing emancipated the role of the computer in business.

With online processing, the organization was suddenly interested in transaction response time and system availability.

Data warehousing

After online transaction processing came data warehousing. Data warehousing caused the disc storage marketplace to explode. Data warehousing enabled analytical processing that had not been previously possible. Data warehousing opened the door to:

- Analytical processing
- The ability to store data historically, something that was not possible before

- The ability to look at data across the corporation rather than look at data by means of applications.

Suddenly, there was a volume of data that had never before been imagined. Even large data warehouses could not hold all the data that appeared.

After data began to be archived, it was recognized that even more data was emerging. The need for bulk storage and the management of that data became a reality.

Database design

In many ways, the evolution of storage media set the stage for the evolution of database design. In the very earliest days, database design was no more complicated than determining what data you were working with and organizing into a data layout. A typical data layout for customer might look like:

- Account number
- Customer name
- Customer address
- Customer telephone number
- Customer gender
- Customer date of birth
- Customer credit card type
- Customer credit card number.

The records created by the earliest computers were limited to 80 columns, not leaving much room for lengthy fields of data.

Linked data

Next in the evolution of database design came the creation of linked (or related) records. Because records had a limited length at that time, so not much data could be placed on a record, linking different kinds of records became standard practice. In doing so, greater amounts of data could be captured. As a simple example, one record of data would look like:

- Customer
    - Customer account
    - Customer name

……..

And another record would look like:

- Order number
    - Item ordered
    - Customer account

………………….

In such a fashion, the customer information could be linked to the order information made by the customer. The linkage was provided by the inclusion of customer accounts in both records. While linkages were possible, making those linkages dynamically was difficult as long as the data was accessed sequentially. Once the data could be accessed directly, linkages through linked records became a much easier task to accomplish.

Normalization

At about this time, the notion that data should be structured in a normalized manner emerged. Normalization meant that data was to be organized around a central key. In the earliest days of direct data access, there was an emphasis on database design that used minimal space. With the advent of lots of storage and direct data access, online transaction processing soon became a reality. Online processing introduced the need for transaction performance and system availability. One technique for achieving high system performance was through the creation of simple data structures. This was achieved through the denormalization of data structures. Denormalized data processed through the system significantly faster than normalized data.

Data warehouse

With transaction processing came the need for lots of data processing applications. Unfortunately, with the numerous applications of data, it was not easy to look across the corporation and achieve a comprehensive corporate view of data. Soon, the data warehouse became a way to achieve a consolidated corporate view of data.

The data warehouse created a low level of granularity of data that was based on the relational model. The data warehouse integrates data from applications to create a true corporate understanding of data.

A data model lies at the heart of converting data from applications to a data warehouse. The data model projected the state and structure of the corporate understanding of data.

Data marts

Data flows from the data warehouse into data marts, where each department has its own understanding of data. Data marts feed many sorts of analytical applications. Over time, data began to aggregate in the data warehouse. It was noticed that much of the data in the data warehouse became dormant—not used frequently or at all.

From the dormant data in the data warehouse came the practice of archiving data. The data structure was maintained, but the data not being used was archived off the data warehouse. Over time, even the archival data became too voluminous. Then, the archived data was sent to simple bulk storage. In bulk storage, data can still be retrieved electronically if needed.

Notably, one step of database design was not discarded upon an evolution to a later step, for the most part. In other words, if you were designing archival storage, you still had to go through the steps of organizing the keys and attributes of data, identifying records, identifying relationships between records, and so forth.

Data lake

Soon an architectural structure called the data lake appeared. The notion behind the data lake was to collect all of these forms of data into a large collection, place them in storage, and then let the end user do analytics against them.

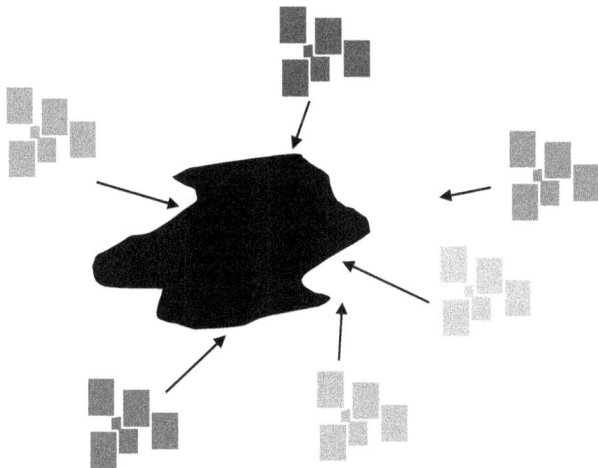

Figure 30: Next came the data lake.

Very shortly, as users and corporations began to implement the data lake, the inadequacies of the data lake began to become apparent:

- Lots and lots of data was put into the data lake.

- As data was put into the data lake, it was not integrated. There was just this big collection of raw data.

- There were scant amounts of metadata collected into the data lake that could be used to direct the user as to the location of the data in the data lake.

- Data in the data lake could not be related efficiently or accurately to other data in the data lake.

- Storing all this data in the data lake was expensive.

Ultimately, no one uses most of the data lake data to any great extent. In short order, the data lake began to hinder information management rather than becoming an asset. The data lake quickly turned into a data swamp.

Data lakehouse

Then, the world began to build data lakehouses. (Note: the terms data lake and data lakehouse sound very similar but have very different meanings and implications.)

The data lakehouse solved the problems of the data lake. The data lakehouse:

- Accommodated all kinds of data
- Provided a metadata directory of where the data resided
- Allowed the data to be joined together
- Mandated that the data be integrated before entering the data lakehouse.

For these reasons, the data lakehouse provided a solid foundation for analytical processing throughout the organization.

Computer evolution

Database design depended indirectly on the computer on which it ran. The earliest computers were a collection of small, slow computers that ran on various machines. At that time, every computer had to have its own unique operating system. Then IBM came out with System 360, which had the ability to share software across computers. The IBM 360 line started what became known as the mainframe computer. The mainframe computer began to dominate the industry and became the de facto standard for many shops.

Compared to today's computers, the mainframe was a low-powered computer. At the time, the mainframe was the most powerful computer around.

The mainframe computer competed with parallel computing, where the workload and data were divided across multiple computers, thus achieving a high level of performance.

Then, one day, the personal computer made its entrance. Personal computers and spreadsheet technology have made computation affordable and available to everyone. Soon, departments began to escape from the mainframe and move much of their business to personal computers. Shortly after the personal computer appeared, small handheld computers arrived.

Then, processing power became available on the cloud.

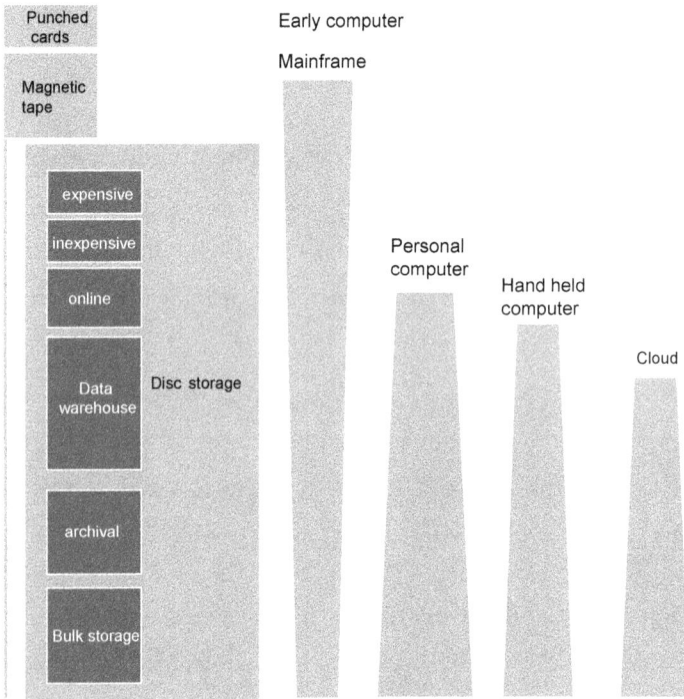

Figure 31: Computer evolution.

Probability of access of data

From the standpoint of database design, a factor that became important was the probability of accessing data. It began to be recognized that the probability of accessing data plays an important role in the placement and structure of data.

The higher the probability of access, the nearer the data needs to be to the user. The lower the probability of access of data, the further the data needs to be to the end user.

The following figure shows that the data that is the most likely to be used is the nearest to the person, and the data that is least likely to be used is the farthest from the user.

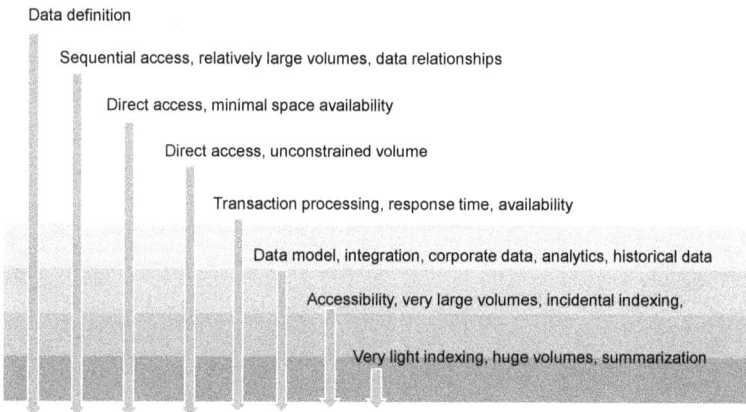

Data definition

Sequential access, relatively large volumes, data relationships

Direct access, minimal space availability

Direct access, unconstrained volume

Transaction processing, response time, availability

Data model, integration, corporate data, analytics, historical data

Accessibility, very large volumes, incidental indexing,

Very light indexing, huge volumes, summarization

Figure 32: The probability of access as a design criteria started after transaction processing became established.

The notion of the probability of access of data being a factor in database design began as volumes of data began to accumulate and transactions needed to run very quickly.

The notion that probability of access began to be a criterion for design started with online transaction processing. Over time, the recognition continued to grow.

Summary

Database design started simply enough. Soon, database design became complicated. Response time, the need for high availability, the requirement to access corporate data, and the need to analyze data all drove the evolution of database design. In addition, database design was driven by the media and computers, which were needed to support the databases.

Chapter 8

Different Kinds of Data

Most people are familiar with structured data. Structured data was the first kind of data that emerged on the scene of computation, and structured data is what people naturally think of when they think of data. Indeed, structured data is still being used, created, and analyzed, and it is some of the most valuable data.

In today's world, other kinds of data find their way into organizations. In particular, there are textual data and analog data, which have very different properties from structured data. The interesting thing about textual data is that:

- There is a lot of it
- Textual data is full of important, business-relevant data
- Almost no one is using it for business value.

A significant amount of value is hidden in analog data. Most people are unaware of the value missing in their decision-making process.

The modern data architect needs to embrace all three kinds of data, not just the structured data in the corporation.

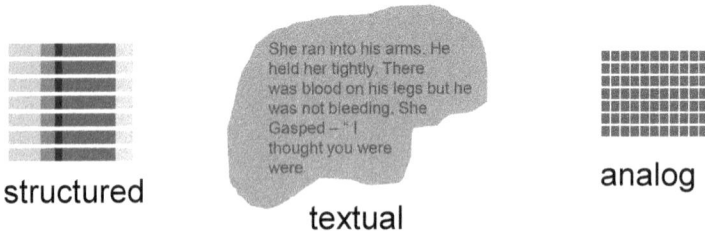

structured

She ran into his arms. He held her tightly. There was blood on his legs but he was not bleeding. She Gasped – "I thought you were were

textual

analog

Figure 33: The data architect needs to be prepared to deal with three kinds of data.

One of the interesting aspects of the three different types of data is that, although they are all forms of data, each has distinct properties. The tools and techniques that work well for one type of data usually do not work well or at all for other types of data. Each type of data has its own set of tools and techniques.

Despite the different properties of the various types of data, all three types of data require an environment that facilitates analysis. The analysis, of course, improves the efficiency and profitability of the corporation.

Structured data

Structured data is data that has a consistent structure for all records contained within it. Structured data is optimized for efficient processing by a computer. Structured data records usually consist of one or more keys and attributes.

Structured data is accessed through an index or an algorithm, depending on the type of data.

In a normalized structured record, the existence of the attribute depends on the key value found in the record. For example, in a customer record, the customer's name and credit rating depend on the customer number. For a product, the product's cost and description depend on the product number.

While the structure of each record in a structured database is identical, the content of each structured record is different. As an example of differing content, look at a database designed for the royal family of England.

One record is for Charles, one record is for Diana, and one record is for Harry. Each record has very different content, even though the structure of all records is the same.

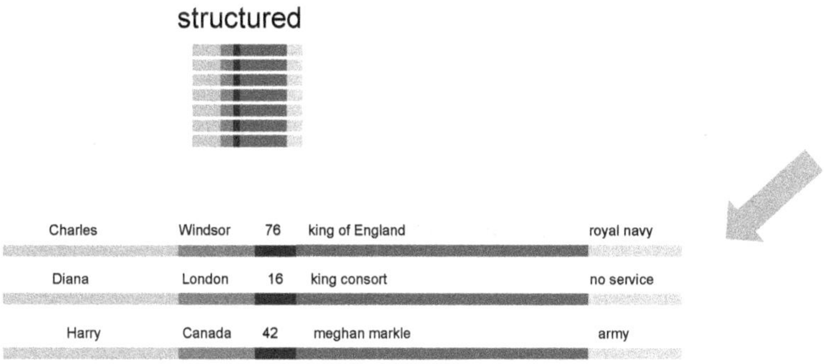

structured

Charles	Windsor	76	king of England	royal navy
Diana	London	16	king consort	no service
Harry	Canada	42	meghan markle	army

Figure 34: The content is different but the structure is the same.

In almost every case, structured records support transaction processing. In some cases, the record is created directly as the result of the execution of a transaction. In other cases, the structured record indirectly supports the transaction database.

structured

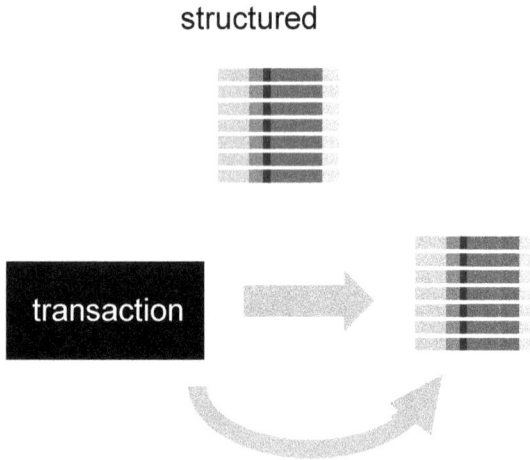

Figure 35: Nearly all structured data comes from transaction processing–either directly or indirectly.

Textual data

The second kind of data the data architect needs to deal with is textual data. Textual data is much more voluminous than structured data. In many cases, extremely valuable data is wrapped in the form of text.

Traditionally, organizations have not done much with textual data.

The issue with textual data is that computers cannot easily read and analyze text. That is because text comes in a completely free-form style that differs from structured data.

Contrast text with structured data. In structured data, the computer knows what a record looks like and has at least some knowledge about every record. Each structured record has the same format and structure. For this reason, the computer can efficiently handle structured data, one record at a time.

The computer does not know textual data. Textual data is free-form, and the computer is not equipped to handle textual data in the same way it handles structured data.

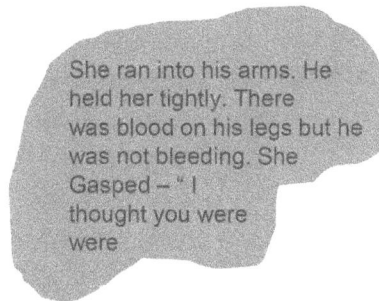

Figure 36: Textual data is completely free form.

Complicating matters in handling text is the fact that with text, there is much extraneous text that needs to be discarded before the computer can even begin to understand it.

The primary reason text is so difficult to handle is that it requires the recognition of not only the text itself, but also its context. Finding and handling text is not easy, but it can be done. Handling and finding the context of text is a different matter altogether. Context is much more difficult to find or infer than the text itself.

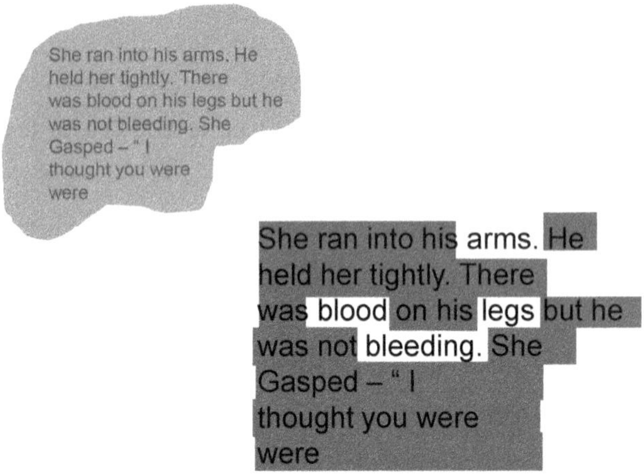

Figure 37: Much of text is extraneous and needs to be discarded.

As a simple example of the importance of understanding the context of text as well as the text itself, consider the meaning of the word "fire." What does the word "fire" mean?

- Fire can mean a conflagration
- Fire can mean the loss of a job
- Fire can mean the pulling of a trigger on a gun.

There are many other meanings of the word *fire*. The truth is that you don't know what is meant by "fire" until you understand the context in which the word is spoken.

The confusion with "fire" is hardly limited to this single word. The need for contextual clarification is evident in many aspects of language.

> *Context is complex and difficult to understand when trying to understand text. Yet context is absolutely and unequivocally essential to the comprehension of text.*

Context is not the only thorny issue. Another issue is the fact that text is found in many different forms. Some of the many places where text is found are:

- The printed page, such as newspapers, books, and reports
- The spoken word, such as in call centers, conversations, and meetings
- On the Internet, such as in customer reviews and advertisements
- On spreadsheets
- In databases
- In email
- In contracts
- In medical records
- Over the telephone.

If you want to analyze text, especially large amounts of text, you must put it through the transformation process. One of the technologies that can facilitate transformation is Textual ETL. Textual ETL reads the raw text, analyzes it, and spits out the results. Textual ETL is simple to use, fast, and inexpensive, requiring no special consultants.

Transformation is a complex process. Many aspects of transformation must be taken into account. Furthermore, many of these aspects are unrelated to one another.

Some of the aspects of transformation include:

- Alternate spelling: Americans spell the word "color." English spell the same word "colour," but it means the same thing.
- Proximity: "Dallas cowboys" refers to a once-great football team. However, "Dallas" by itself refers to a Texas city.
- Many words are extraneous and need to be removed, such as "a," "and," "the," etc.
- Context must be determined. Does "fire" refer to a conflagration? Or does the word "fire" refer to the involuntary loss of a job.
- The digits "999-999-9999" refer to an American telephone number.

Many other aspects of language need to be resolved before a computer can codify text.

The output from the transformation process is a standard database. The database contains (at a minimum) the following types of data:

- Identification of the source of the text. This is necessary in case clarification is ever needed regarding the interpretation made.

- Location of the word in the text. This is necessary in case there is ever a need to revisit and determine exactly which word has been chosen for analysis.
- The word that has been selected
- The context of the word that has been selected.

It is noted that many other aspects of transformation can be captured as well. Some of them include:

- Higher levels of contextualization
- Degree of contextualization
- Identification of the algorithm used in transformation.

Analog data

The third type of data that the data architect needs to handle is analog data. Analog data is data that is generated by a machine. A typical usage of analog data generation is when a machine produces a part. The part is measured, the machine identification is noted, the time of day is noted, and the operator of the machine and the lot number being manufactured is noted. Throughout the day, the machine sits there and spews out data for every product that is produced.

Throughout the day, many products are produced. As long as the part that is being produced meets the standards of the organization, the record that has been produced is of little or no value. When a part is produced that is outside the boundaries of the organization's standards, the record of the part becomes of great interest. The record produced provides clues as to why the malfunction occurred. Some of the things that are examined are:

- Was the input material defective?
- Did the machine need maintenance?
- Did the operator do something incorrectly?

Managing analog data is challenging because many devices generate analog data. Some of the devices produce data that is of interest to the corporation. The analog data generated by many devices is not of any significant interest to the organization.

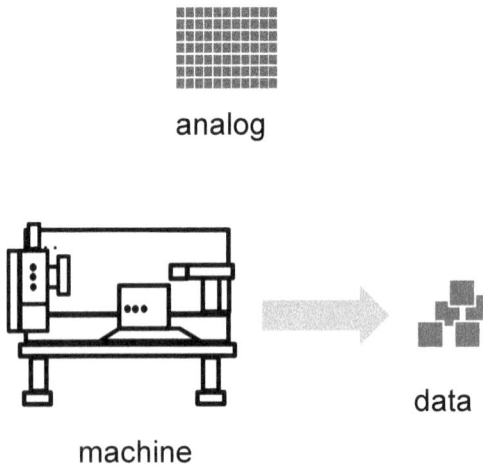

Figure 38: Analog data is generated by a machine.

Although analog data is usually structured and therefore, simpler to handle than textual data, the data that is of interest must be separated from the data that is not useful. This can be a lot of work!

Given the volume of generated data, it makes no sense to store and manage all the generated data. Instead, it makes sense to only store those records that indicate some unusual condition. The problem is finding those records that are of interest. For example, every time a part is manufactured, the following data is captured:

- Time of the event
- Machine identification that produced the product
- Item that was produced
- Identification of the items that were produced
- Operator of the machine.

Of course, many other kinds of data could have been produced due to the machine's operation. This is simply an example of what analog data might look like.

Time	machine	item	operator
1:14	AX235	coupler	J Smith
1:16	LM90	router	K Dawdler
1:19	AX114	gasket	M Tomlinson
1:23	AX235	coupler	J Smith
1:26	RW009	Cam	T Jackson
1:30	AX235	coupler	D Hollebeke
1:26	LM90	router	D Hardy

Figure 39: A simple example.

Much of the data produced by a machine has little or no business value. Some of the data produced by analog data has great value.

The data that has great value is the data that has been captured during an "event." An event may be the production of a part that is outsized. An event may be a record of events when a lightning bolt hits the plant. An event may be when a new operator takes over a machine.

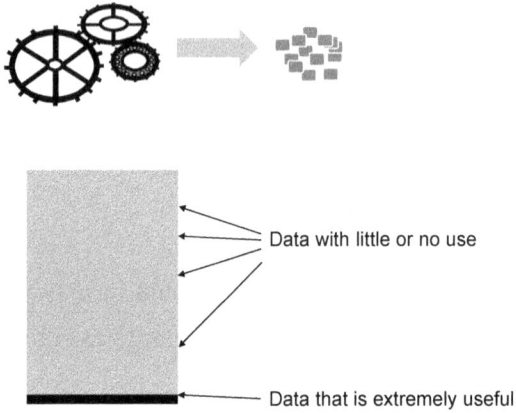

Figure 40: The issue with analog data.

At this point, it is normal to ask, "What is the dividing line between these two kinds of data, data with little value and data with great value?"

How can the designer tell the difference between these two types of data? The distillation algorithm makes the difference between these two data types. The distillation algorithm reads all the data and ferrets the data with great value. Data that has no (or low) value goes into one pile. Data that has great value goes into another pile.

The distillation algorithm can take several forms:

- **Manual inspection**. For example, there is a car robbery in a parking lot. Suppose there is a video of the parking lot. The police sit down to view the videotape and gather the necessary information. They sit down for a long time. This is tedious because someone from the police department has to review hours of footage to find a single 60-second segment. The worst that can happen is that the reviewer looks away and misses the important 60 seconds. In this case, the interesting tape will never be found.

- **Threshold approach**. A more effective approach is to monitor what you are looking for to determine a threshold. Once the measurement exceeds the threshold, a record is written. However, not all data can be defined with a threshold, and a threshold that is too low causes "false positives" and too high may miss events.

- **Dual threshold approach**. With a lower and upper bound, the crossing creates the writing of an event record when either of these boundaries is crossed.

- **Time zoning**. All records from a specific point in time are retained until a later point in time arrives. This approach works whenever there is an expected time for an event to occur. However, there may be an event that occurs outside of the time zone. If so, the record of the event will be missed.

- **Sampling**. A sample of data is recorded at regular intervals. The sampling approach is not really designed to capture an event. The sampling approach is used to identify trends.

Summary

As the volume of data increases, the business value contained in the data decreases. This paradox, then, is one of the greatest challenges the data architect faces.

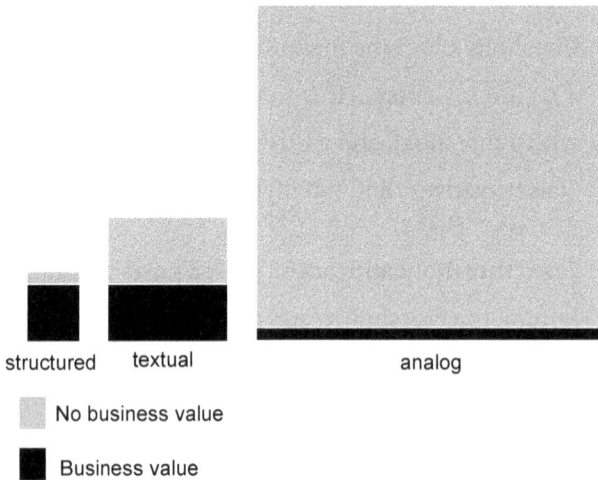

Figure 41: The disparities in both the business value and the volumes of data must be accounted for by the data architect.

The data architect needs to manage three basic types of data. There is structured data. There is textual data, and there is analog data. All three types of data have their own challenges.

Chapter 9

Bulk Storage

In the beginning, storage was created in units called bits. A bit could take on the value of a one or a zero. The bit was controlled by the intersection of three wires that fit through the bit. The current passed through the wires controlled the bit's status, 1 or 0. The individual bits formed what is called a "byte."

In the early days, bits were beaded by hand, much like a necklace. Very quickly, the notion of manual storage beading faded. There simply was too much demand for storage. There were not enough beaders in the world to keep up with the demand for storage. In addition, manual beading was prohibitively expensive.

Soon, the world turned to automated storage manufacturing. In the very early days, storage was expensive. At the same time, the speed and sophistication of computers were also advancing.

As the industry matured, the cost of storage dropped, and storage began to be manufactured on a widespread basis. Whereas once storage was the limiting factor in computing, computing power became the limiting factor. In a few years, the amount of storage began to be much greater than the computing power. Storage was much less of a factor in what could be done with a computer. Once, having a megabyte (1,000,000 bytes) of storage was an accomplishment. In a later day, having a petabyte (1,000,000,000,000,000 bytes) of storage was a reality.

As the volume of data and storage progressed, it was noticed that not all data was being used, either frequently or at all. Soon data began to divide itself into three categories:

- **Actively used data**. Data being used on a daily basis to run the business.
- **Semi-dormant data**. Data being used occasionally to make strategic decisions.
- **Dormant data**. Data not being used at all.

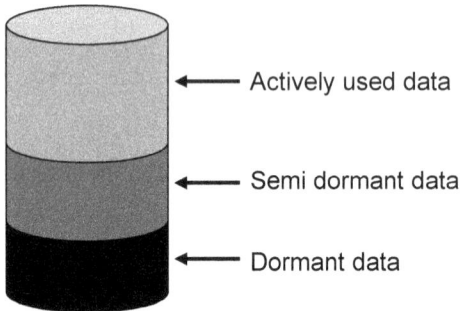

Figure 42: Over time, data began to divide itself into these categories.

The challenges with the rise in the volume of data then became:

- Managing all of the data

- Managing the expense of the data
- Finding data when you needed it
- Running queries efficiently.

Issues

It was noticed that the bill for storage began to be a real issue. Even though the unit price of storage had plummeted, the total rate of consumption of storage was far greater than the rate of decrease of the unit price of storage. As a result, the amount of money paid for storage and the impact of the volume of storage on processing became a real concern. This was especially true as people began storing their data in the cloud. In addition to the issue of the expense of data, an accompanying issue was the problem of finding data in a sea of data. Having huge amounts of data effectively hid the data being used. If the large amounts of data did not hide data, it certainly made the search for data less efficient and more expensive.

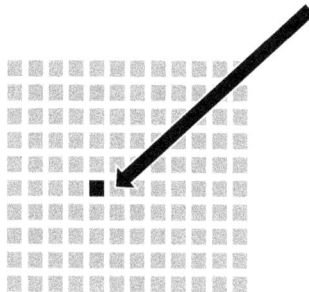

Figure 43: Data that you are looking for hides behind mountains of data that you are not looking for.

The issue with the growing amount of semi-dormant and dormant data was that the problem became worse each day. Over time, the problem grew and grew, never improving.

Different forms of storage

It then became apparent that merely storing data in a single type of storage was not a good idea. Of course, the vendor preferred the client to do that because it generated more revenue for the vendor. A much better idea was to place data in different forms of storage.

The form of storage was designed to accommodate the particular needs of the data. High-performance storage was used for high-performance transaction processing. Mid-level storage was used for analytics. In addition, bulk storage was used for data that might be used in the future, but for purposes presently unknown.

There is a question that arises:

Shouldn't dormant data just be thrown away?

The answer is that if the probability of future usage is truly zero, it should be thrown away.

If there is ever an unforeseen circumstance where the data might be needed, then the data should be kept.

Probability of access

Another way to look at the division of data across different platforms is by the probability of access.

Data with a high probability of access should be stored in expensive, high-performance storage. Data with a moderate probability of access should be stored in mid-performance storage. Data with a low probability of access should be stored in bulk storage.

Periodically, the data should be audited and data should be removed from one level of storage and sent to the next based on the probability of access to the data.

The auditing can be based on many different types of criteria:

- The age of the data
- The usage of the data
- The contents of the data.

If the audit shows that the data is misplaced, then data should be removed from one level and added to another level or deleted all together.

On occasion, the probability of accessing data changes, and data that once had a low probability of access suddenly has a higher probability of access. This change occurs infrequently, but it does happen occasionally.

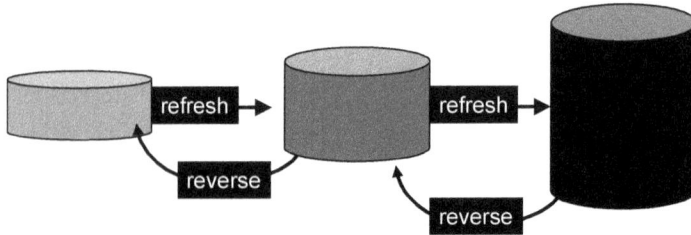

Figure 44: On occasion, there is a reverse flow of data when the probability of access changes.

When the probability of access of data changes, there needs to be a reverse migration of the data.

Accessing bulk storage

Once data is placed into bulk storage, it does not mean it is not electronically accessible. Bulk storage can be accessed electronically. However, bulk storage is not designed for efficient access. Accessing bulk storage is:

- Awkward to engineer
- Slow to process
- Involves lots and lots of data.

Data sent to bulk storage does not mean that it is inaccessible.
It simply means that when data is sent to bulk storage, it will require effort to locate the data.

One way to increase the efficiency of finding data in bulk storage is to create what is known as "incidental indexes."

When indexes are built, they are typically created to locate a single record. There is a reason why a single record must be sought:

- The record represents a bank balance
- The record represents an airline reservation
- The record represents an airplane part.

However, there is no such requirement for bulk storage. Furthermore, in bulk storage, there is much, much more data. For these reasons, an incidental index does not specify the location of a single record. Instead, the incidental index represents a broad classification of data.

Typical of the types of data that make up an incidental index might be:

- Year, date
- Country produced
- Product line
- Company sold through.

The purpose of the incidental index is not to find a single record but to weed out data that does not belong to the search, thereby streamlining the search through bulk data.

Incidental indexes divide bulk storage into broad classifications of data.

Summary

Over time, large amounts of data start to collect. Some of the data is useful and some of the data is not useful. The data needs to be divided into sections based on the probability of usage. The effect of dividing the data is that the division reduces the cost of storage and speeds the time of query processing.

Chapter 10

The Catalog

We love to save documents.

We have saved documents since the first love letters were written on papyrus. We save documents of every sort. We keep contracts, medical records, tax documents, receipts, presentations, manuals, memos, and meeting notes, just to name a few. We download countless documents from our emails as our Downloads directory fills up. We create Word documents, Excel spreadsheets, PowerPoint presentations, PDF files, and images, and might put them in our documents folder. We create folders and subfolders on our computer with specific names for better document organization. We also save them on file servers to share with others within the company. Our desire to save documents is carefully instilled in our schools and offices, with a nod to our highly litigious society. We are told, "Just save it because storage is cheap and you might need it later. You never know!"

We have documents stored on every computer, phone, and email account, and with decades of cloud storage behind us, we have stored our documents online. Between Microsoft Office Online, Google Docs, and other cloud storage services, our documents now reside on servers located worldwide.

With the advent of data lakes, companies have been given the promise that "We can store all of your documents and data in one place, cheaper and safer than your company can." So, companies have started saving even more, dumping more data and more documents into these data lakes.

There are inherent issues with saving all these documents everywhere. If you're wondering what issues exist, watch any episode of "Hoarders." The first issue should become clearer. We are saving mountains of worthless junk in the hope that one piece might be useful in the future. The fact is that so much of that junk has actual value if it is stored properly and can be found efficiently when needed.

Since these documents contain potentially valuable business data, this data should be part of a company's data architecture, but quite often, it is shelved for later or ignored altogether because of its unstructured nature. The data architect dismisses documents as part of their job because the data is randomly dispersed throughout the company, and the job is too big.

So, what is the solution? The solution is the same as it is at your local library. The solution is organization. Consider the amount of useful information available at your local library. If we took the same approach at the library as we do with current data lakes and file storage, we would throw all the books into a room and say, "See, our storage is cheap. You can find the information you need when you want it in the future. We have stored it all in the book room. By the way, we only charge you for looking for your book, reading pages of any book, or when you check out the book to actually use your information."

Using data terms, throwing your documents into a "book room" is called, "Extract, Load, and Transform." It is *always* a poor choice unless you enjoy trudging through a data swamp!

The need for a catalog

The correct way to find your data is the same way you find your books at the local library. You go to the card catalog. You first search for the category of information you are looking to find according to a cataloging system called the Dewey Decimal System. You then have a quicker time finding the books or information you need and their location in the library. Finding data in your immense repository of documents requires a similar catalog. The catalog, and the creation of the catalog, should be part of the company's data architecture.

You create a catalog so that you can find specific documents and their location on the proverbial shelf. You create a catalog so that you can find other documents that are related to the one you are looking for so that you have supporting documentation. You create a catalog because you don't remember the exact words, figures, or phrases in the document, but you recall saving it. You remember the general gist of the document that you are looking for. A catalog makes this search possible and feasible. This is why we use the Dewey Decimal System to find the books we need on the countless library shelves.

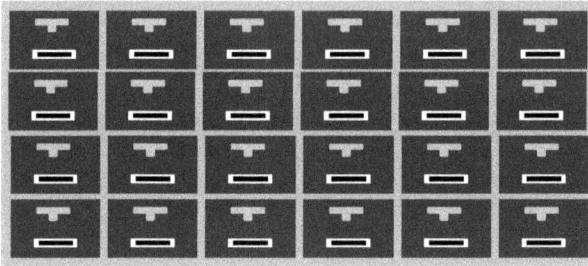

Figure 45: A card catalog for corporate documents.

Suppose you are looking for a quote from Winston Churchill. That seems like that might be considered "General Knowledge." In the card catalog, we could begin with "Class 000: Computer science, information, and general works." From there, we look under "010 Bibliographies," and then "012 Bibliographies of Individuals" to find what someone else wrote on Winston Churchill. We might get the quote from there. Another route would be to look under "080 Quotations," and then "082 Collections in English" to find a book on quotations of global leaders or even British Prime Ministers. The catalog would provide a list of all books, along with a brief synopsis of each, allowing you to quickly find a few that might meet your needs. The

Dewey Decimal System would point you directly to the shelf location.

So, if we are going to create a catalog for our company's documents, what does this catalog look like? Just like at the library, your catalog begins with context. When we go to a library's card catalog, we look first by context. Textual documents are based on a subject of some sort. They could contain a series of subjects, but at a minimum, they have at least one. This subject is the context area of the document. The information, words, phrases, and diagrams in that document have meaning in that field of context. There are specific words and phrases in the documents that can be classified within that context. A more generalized area further classifies these classifications. These generalized areas, classifications, and specific words and phrases can be set up in a Taxonomy. This taxonomy is joined with other taxonomies, along with a series of rules on handling text, patterns, names, and sentiment, to create what we will call a Nexus. Consider a Nexus to be the fully classified, multi-level search criteria for finding your documents. This discrete-level classification system provides users with a means to search across multiple levels, without needing to know the exact words in the document.

Let's say you are looking for an internal memo from a few years ago that references possible changes to the maintenance procedures of a Ford Ranger transmission shifter cable. If you simply dump all your documents into a data lake or spread them throughout your company without classification or a catalog, you will not be able to find that document. Where would you begin? Where is that document, or where was that document?

If your company decided just to consolidate your documents in a data lake or on a file server, you could do a general search, but you need to have the exact wording in the document or the exact title of the document to find the specific document for which you are looking. Therefore, searching for "Ford Ranger transmission shifter cable" would yield no results, but would require a significant amount of time and real money. So, you reduce the "search phrase" to find your document. You might just search for "Ford." This approach will not work because it is too general and lacks context. Searching through the number of documents that involve the word Ford would be overwhelming. Your company has documents on Ford Cars, Henry Ford, President Gerald Ford, and Ford dealerships. If you search for 'Ranger,' you will find documents related to the following areas: truck documents, Texas Rangers Baseball, New York Rangers Ice Hockey, US Army Special Forces, and US Forest Ranger. You could search on transmission shifter cable, but again, you might get no documents because it is not in the title of the saved document, or you will get tens of thousands of documents relating to transmission shifter cables, from maintenance documents to design schematics to installation standards for every year of every type of vehicle your company handles.

Your company will spend more time and money searching for this document without a positive result because its title was "Maintenance (1)." On the third page, it had "Transmission shift cable Ford Ranger 1997-2005, Explorer Sport Trac" in the text of the document. A second document, created three years later because the first one was lost, called "Updated Cable Maintenance," just referenced the part number "F77Z-7E395-LB" in the document without any of the text "Ford Ranger transmission shifter cable."

The fact that you cannot find this document does not alter the fact that you still need it. You need this document to mitigate a lawsuit, for a business plan, or for a training module you are building. You will not find the document. You were fighting a losing battle from the start because you only have human memory to go on instead of a plan. If your textual data is not part of the company's data architecture, you will repeat history, waste your employees' time, build frustration, and recreate the wheel. You need a plan!

A catalog is the plan that the data architect can implement.

Let's say you've implemented a catalog and want to search for a specific document. Using an internal chatbot interface, a knowledge graph, or a standard database, you can search for "Ranger" or "truck," limited by a "shifter cable" or "shift cable," and show me "memos" or "maintenance documents." A short list of documents, including the two you can use, will appear for you to click on and review.

What was an impossible task becomes quick and efficient because the words, phrases, and titles of this document have been given context and classification. This catalog of your documents is a searchable database of key terms and phrases within a defined context for specified documents. Building the catalog is not a small or easy undertaking for many reasons:

- It takes planning.
- It requires buy-in from top brass to rank-and-file employees.
- It is not free.
- People are not great organizers of documents.
- People save a lot of junk (especially documents).
- People have terrible memories (about what is in the documents or where they were stored).
- Big tech has built the hardware platforms to allow for unlimited hardware resources to be thrown at bad planning and has convinced Engineers that this is a valid business solution.
- Big tech has convinced engineers and computer scientists that "Extract Load Transform" is the same as "Extract Transform Load".
- Engineers and computer scientists assure business decision-makers that "Extract Load Transform" is the same as "Extract Transform Load".
- People are given unrestricted "cheap" storage to not organize their documents.
- Big tech assures business decision-makers that their cloud storage and data lake platforms are more secure, less expensive, and more efficient than traditional platforms.

This new process is called "Extract Classify Load (ECL)." This new process is not the same as "Extract, Transform, Load" (ETL), which is typically used for storing data in a data warehouse; however, it shares a similar approach. This new process aims to rectify the misguided and destructive "Extract Load Transform" process, which is ineffective and serves as the basis for turning your data lake into a data swamp. "Extract, Classify, Load (ECL)" provides a data architect with the tools to incorporate vast amounts of textual data into the company's data architecture.

Extract Classify Load (ECL)

ECL is the creation of the catalog. It involves extracting text from a document, classifying key contextualized data from the text, and loading those classifications into the catalog.

The ECL process has two parts. The first part addresses the current textual data that exists in your data swamp and is stored in your file storage solutions throughout your company. The second part addresses new and updated documents that will be added to your data lake. For the first part of implementing the Extract Classify Load (ECL) process, you need to know where your files reside. If corporate files are stored in these widespread locations or centralized, that procedure needs to be established and implemented. Much like placing books on the shelves in a library, thought and agreement should be used to locate your documents. For this to work, you need top-brass support and rank-and-file buy-in. Your front-line employees are the people who create and curate most of the important documents in your company. If they recognize the value in saving documents in organized locations for later retrieval, you will achieve success. If you cannot give them a valid business reason for their extra effort, your swamp will grow and decimate your company's chances of finding this important data source, much less of making use of it.

Extract Classify Load (ECL) requires planning and structure for how and where files will be stored.

If, as a company, you have a file or folder system that requires certain documents to be saved in certain areas, you are among the minority, but that is ideal. This allows a Nexus to be established for documents within that folder structure, which can be applied to all current and future documents.

If you are running a job shop, all the files for a job are often placed in one directory and then organized in a standard way using subdirectories. If this is standardized and followed for each job, a process and Nexus can be established for specific subfolders. This will help contextualize the files as the catalog classification process is used.

If you do not have any current process for storing files, which is the case in the majority of companies, then the classification Nexus will need to be a little wider to account for the myriad subjects of your documents. It is a good idea to establish a standard procedure for storing future files, allowing for more accurate classification and cataloging. Once again, this should be done with the support of employees from all areas and all levels. This is part of your data governance procedures.

The second part of the ECL process deals with new and changed documents. As new files are placed into specified file servers or data lake file systems, a system trigger must be activated on those files to classify the data within them, allowing for easy retrieval when needed. Major data lake platforms have these micro functions readily available for implementation. As files are updated, they should be rerun against the classification procedure. This update provides both a history of the file and its current state, allowing it to be found based on its historical information.

Metadata

Classification is the process of extracting searchable key points from each of your company's documents. This data is called metadata. Metadata for our catalog is data in the form of a searchable database that directs search and reporting engine users to the relevant document.

Images, videos, PDFs, Word documents, and sound files are unstructured data. They cannot be easily searched or quickly found. They are just data that we save in hopes of using it later. How do we find these files? To find the files, we added searchable data. We add tags. We add metadata. This is essentially the "C" part of ECL.

For a picture, we will add a title, descriptive words, a date, a location, and a brief description. For a video, we add actors, directors, characters, and descriptions for specific timestamps within that video. These various tags transform this unstructured data into semi-structured data. This metadata allows search engines to find these files.

When dealing with a catalog, classification requires a more substantial step than the simple metadata extraction we have done in the past. For an actual Extract, Classify, and Load process to work, we need to have a context for that textual document. This multilevel dictionary, this Nexus, provides a roadmap for what internal textual metadata we will extract and categorize, utilizing multiple, broadening levels. The reason for this is to ensure that the list of files a searcher needs to review is the most concise and relevant, including the appropriate file. When we look for a document about President Gerald Ford, one that never actually says President or Gerald, we should be able to find that document because the document was run against a Nexus where "Ford" was part of a classification of Presidents, in an area of US Leaders, in a taxonomy of Leaders. We should not be burdened with searching through non-related documents about the Ford Rangers or the Betsy Ford Clinic.

When ECL is run against documents, it extracts the standard tag metadata that other unstructured data yield when turned into

THE CATALOG • 117

semi-structured data. If necessary, you extract File Name, File Type, Authors, Locations, File Locations, Versions, and other attribute information. The key difference in ECL is that it also extracts contextually classified information about the subject matter in the documents. You get the location of each piece of data within the document. You get page numbers, paragraphs, and context or meaning. This enables node database searches, heat maps, and direct access to the data you need within large documents, eliminating the need to read every page to find it.

When you want to know what disease the doctor thinks the patient displayed during a past visit, you need more than "it is in the SOAP Notes for the patient." Please note that the relevant information is located in the second sentence of the third paragraph in the July 15th note. The text file and voice file from which it was transcribed are available here.

The catalog enables you to search for a disease in a patient's records across all text documents, returning all instances of these diseases along with additional metadata on who, when, and where the disease was stated. You may think this can be found within a standard Electronic Medical Record (EMR) program today. If you have worked with doctors using an EMR, you know that they do not always click on the items on the screen that correspond to what they dictate regarding a visit. The real important information is usually in the transcribed notes.

One might ask, "Why don't we just keep all of the text as metadata? Isn't text searchable?" Text indexing of documents has been used for decades, but it is not an efficient way to search for the documents you need. The Nexus, established by the company's data governance body, along with the assistance of certain AI tools, provides guidelines on the key elements of our documents. We do not need all of the text. We need key points of the text that have been contextualized into standard areas and classifications so that anyone can find the documents they need, regardless of the order or dialect of the original words or phrases.

The metadata is the searchable result of classifying textual data as part of the ECL process. This metadata becomes the basis for the catalog. The catalog serves as your multi-dimensional Dewey Decimal System for locating documents within your global file repository.

Summary

Textual data has business value, but historically, the monumental task of consolidating, searching, and using our textual data has been too overwhelming for data architects to consider taking on the challenge. The use of foundational data governance procedures, curated Nexuses, micro-functions built into data storage platforms, and event-based file management software can overcome this monumental initial challenge and allow our textual data to become part of our data architecture and to be an asset to our business instead of being the sludge that propagates our current data swamps.

Chapter 11

Architecture Support

The setup of the data architecture determines how effectively your data, whether textual, structured, or machine-generated, will be utilized. Thought and planning are essential when setting up the storage, organization, and management of your data. Dumping your data into a hole and throwing bigger shovels at it to find your data when you need it does not work. This is similar to setting up a data lake, with the promise that the platform has as many shovels as you want. Collecting data for later use without understanding or controlling the extraction process, then loading that data into a repository such as a data lake, and subsequently attempting to transform the data into something useful, guarantees long-term failure.

Extract, Load, Transform does not work. As the amount and size of your data and files grow exponentially, the cost in resources and cash itself grows even quicker. This is terrible for your growing business, but great for the platforms that propose ELT as a viable solution. ETL for all data, as well as ECL for textual data, are viable architectural solutions. This only happens when you put a filter or funnel at the entry point of your data lake. This entry point is called a data lakehouse.

Figure 46: The data lakehouse.

With cloud-based technology, scalability, retrieval, integration, and security can be implemented and managed architecturally:

- **Scalability**. Allowing your most important documents to reside haphazardly on your employees' hard drives is not a sound plan. It is not secure. It is not scalable. It is not retrievable or usable at the enterprise level. Architecture needs centralized storage options. This can be done with traditional file servers, but these might not be the most efficient in today's world as they do not allow scalability and growth. The other option is cloud-based storage. This solution allows scalability. With cloud-based storage, as you need more storage in your repository, you add more resources.

- **Retrieval**. If all your files are stored in centralized storage and classified before they are added, then you can retrieve the files from any attached device. Planning needs to take into account how often the files will be accessed. On rented platforms, you pay more for files that are accessed more frequently and less for archived files. This is due to a few real business reasons. Most of your files are stored as Binary Large Objects (BLOBs) on cloud storage. These reduce the physical size of the file but makes it much less accessible. They need to be extracted and transformed into a format that allows them to be read. This is an expensive process in terms of computer resources. Files that are updated or accessed frequently cannot be stored as BLOBs because they need to remain in their native format to avoid the transformation process.

- **Integration**. Textual files that are accessible as part of your data repositories and cataloged through data governance as part of your data architecture can be used as data sources. These data sources direct employees and management to valuable information about customers, products, the business environment, and corporate culture, which will help them make better business decisions. Saving data for data's purpose is idiotic! If data cannot be used and integrated into your business decisions, it wastes time, money, and resources. Have a plan for what data will be saved, used, and integrated into your data architecture, and follow the plan! Teach your employees because it is important. Train them on that plan and reward them for following it properly.

- **Security**. This one seems debatable in light of the recent acts of data theft, ransom, and compromise. This can be attributed to the fact that cyber attacks have increased every week for the past few decades, often led by criminal organizations, hacktivist groups, foreign countries, and internal employees. When asked why he robbed banks, Willie Sutton, the famous 1930s bank robber, simply replied, "Because that's where the money is." Putting all of our data in one "bank" makes it much more attractive to rob. Robbery today takes on many forms. Examining our data, we find that improperly updating, stealing, erasing, and holding data ransom are standard practices among these criminals. Your data architecture must protect your data.

If you have a data architecture that supports scalability, retrieval, integration, and security, you can begin using that data for analysis. Analysis remains a major purpose of having that data. Analysis of structured data accounts for almost 95% of our traditional business decisions. Analysis of machine-generated data requires the creation of machine learning and statistical algorithms to determine if a process is "out of control" or if a machine needs human attention. Analysis of textual data can take the form of identifying specific documents, ranging from contracts to maintenance schedules. It can be used in small and large language models to create chatbots. This can be done with a catalog and a proper ECL process. Textual analysis can take the form of Voice of the Customer, which involves sentiment analysis, keyword analysis, and basket analysis. This can be done if the data has been saved with the correct metadata on who, what, when, where, and how the data was collected. This can provide valuable insight into why customers choose to use your products or services. It can give detailed, actionable suggestions on improving those relationships, retaining customers, and attracting new ones. This can only be done if the architecture allows for data models that include text-mining capabilities.

Constant maintenance

As technology and the business environment change, your architecture will also need to change. These updates should be part of the continual maintenance plan for your data architecture. This does not mean that a technology change should mandate a complete architecture overhaul. The original architecture should have enough flexibility to be modified and maintained as needs change. The data architecture should have a core that can expand and grow. New hardware and software technologies should not be the basis for your data architecture. They should enable your architecture to become more efficient and align with your business needs.

The architecture should serve the business needs.

The architecture should enable the creation of data models that deliver business value, supporting informed decisions and strategy. The architecture should consider the physical geography of the source systems, the reporting and analysis needs of your employees, and the cost of delivering data to the requesting users.

Maintenance costs must be factored into your architecture setup. Each of the data storage and access options has different startup, maintenance, and opportunity costs. If you only focus on capital costs, your plan will fail. Consider our road system. It is expensive to build a road, but we allocate the initial cost for surveying, land acquisition, equipment, and road construction from our capital budget. Placement of the road means that you did not put it somewhere else. Not using this other pathway might mean you miss out on opportunities for potential businesses, homes, or resources in that other road location. This might be rectified with another capital cost, though. Once the road is put into use, if it is not maintained constantly, it will become filled with potholes and eventually become dangerous, even unusable. If the road is extremely congested, you may need to consider widening the road or adjusting the physical lanes to accommodate the traffic patterns. If you do not have a maintenance budget to accompany each capital expenditure, you have guaranteed an end-of-life for your road.

The same goes for your data. If you allocate your capital budget to purchase, set up, and implement the hardware and software necessary for your initial data architecture, you also need to have a complementary maintenance budget to support the ongoing operation, maintenance, expansion, security, and utilization of that architecture as your business evolves or changes.

Your data architect has two major maintenance costs. The first is to maintain the existing architecture with regard to physical hardware, networks, storage, data flow, APIs, architectural expansion, and security. The second major maintenance cost involves data integrity, specifically addressing policies related to governance, archival and removal of data, integration with external data sources and new systems of record, and updating and verifying both new and existing data flows and data streams.

Maintenance costs are constant. They are constant in the fact that they grow. They are constant in the fact that they are needed. They are constant in the fact that they must be part of the corporate annual budget. If they are not part of the original budget and plan, your company's use of data as part of your competitive strategy will not be realized.

Movement across the architecture

Your choice of data management systems helps determine how your data flows throughout your company. Whether you choose a centralized monolithic data warehouse, a series of data marts, a data lake, a data lakehouse, a peer-to-peer system, or a hybrid management system will dictate how you physically store your data. With a data-fabric-based architecture, a series of data meshes, or a decentralized API-based microservices architecture, the movement of data across that architecture will be further dictated. Having the proper network infrastructure to allow timely data movement is paramount.

Planning your data architecture and selecting the actual data management systems helps you determine where to place your data. Proper placement of your data is crucial, especially your textual data. If your users require access to sets of documents, your architecture should enable the movement of key files from archival to active storage, thereby reducing actual costs. As documents reach the end of their usefulness, archival and removal processes must be established and implemented. This type of data maintenance should be part of your architecture's design and maintenance plan.

Physical data management options significantly impact the total costs of your data architecture. In-house storage on company servers, in-house cloud environments, hybrid environments, and rented platforms on remote clouds each have their own advantages and disadvantages. When you consider how hardware, employee, per-use access, opportunity, setup, maintenance, and security costs differ with each solution, you need to justify why you are using that solution. It is often a good idea to consider that a mix of these solutions might be your best option for the physical and logical architecture. High-access data in a cloud environment may not be the most cost-effective solution due to the high per-use costs. If you choose local data management solutions, off-site access and availability might pose a real cost. If you rely on your in-house hardware, you will miss out on updates and opportunities that remote platforms offer. If you rely on remote platforms solely, your per-use costs will skyrocket, and you will be at the mercy of the platform's ever-changing pricing models. As your data progresses through its life cycle, you may consider establishing a physical architecture that enables key data to be transferred to the most suitable platforms, maximizing the utilization of that data for informed business decisions at lower costs in retrieval and integration time, as well as financial expenses.

The movement of data within your architecture requires bandwidth. Advancements in wireline, wireless, and cellular phone data networks have enabled the transfer of greater amounts of data among devices; however, this transfer is never entirely free. Either you are paying internally for network usage or externally for every bit transferred. You pay in money, time, or resources if you do not have a physical storage plan that accurately mirrors your data usage. Status access requirements for your data on reporting also lend to the need for proper planning. Requirements for real-time data aggregation mean that the source systems, the ETL processes, the cataloging processes, and the logical storage of the resultant data will stress the computers and networks. Data architects will often find themselves embroiled in a series of corporate political battles, where data and processes take precedence. Extraction takes time. Cleaning and transforming the data takes time. Loading data into a data warehouse, data mart, data lake, or weaving it into your data fabric requires time and resources. As you build, expand, and maintain your data architecture, these delays in moving data across your company must be taken into account.

Periodic auditing

Data is dirty. Big data is even dirtier. Even with a proven ETL process, data can still degrade over time. This degeneration happens for many reasons. The people in your company change. The data governance is not shared with new employees. The data these employees enter into source systems becomes something different than what was originally intended. As this new, improperly entered data propagates through your architecture, your reports may not accurately reflect the historical trends, actual trends, or even real-time information they are supposed to represent. Data governance falls under the umbrella of data architecture. Training new employees on systems of record reinforces accurate internal data.

Most systems have text or memo fields to allow for a more detailed explanation of meetings, products, or customer interactions. You will find that as needs grow but systems do not, these memo fields hold the data you need to make productive business decisions. The unstructured textual data entered into these source systems should be added to your data architecture by adding the data to your contextual catalog with the appropriate metadata. This transforms your unstructured textual data into searchable semi-structured data. Periodic auditing of your source systems, conducted through interviews with employees, customers, and users, enables you to better understand where important textual data resides and the types of data being entered into those fields.

External data feeds from social media platforms, APIs, and partner systems frequently change, often without prior notice. The meaning of the main fields you use might remain the same or change based on who entered the data. Your company may not have control over what data is being entered, and this contaminated data needs to be cleaned before it propagates through your internal systems. New fields and new APIs are added to data sources containing the actual business value data for your decision-makers. Your company is paying for this data, and it clogs down your networks. However, you will miss this data unless you do periodic audits.

Textual data also changes over time. The terms used in your catalog need to be updated as their meanings change. Context is key. Words, phrases, and especially acronyms that had a single meaning last year will have a completely different meaning this year. New idioms, terms, and phrases become mainstream every year, and these should be added to your catalog. Your contextual catalog must reflect these changes to accurately capture customer sentiment, document context, and meeting notes, ensuring that they accurately reflect the context and meaning of what was said at the time it was stated, rather than relying solely on the exact words used. This will make the text searchable over time. You do not need to go back through old textual documents and add these terms because they were not terms in the past, but they are terms of the current times.

Summary

As new technologies become available, review your architecture to determine if significant efficiencies can be achieved by utilizing these technologies. As advances in computing power, networks, Deep Learning (DL), Machine Learning (ML), and Artificial Intelligence (AI) continue, you may find that modifications to parts of your data architecture may allow for better use of your data.

Saving data just because you can, for possible use in the future, is not good business. Data should be evaluated before it is saved to your architecture. Data should be cataloged before it is added to your architecture. Data should be cleaned before it becomes part of your historical record. Data should be evaluated for its actual business use and value to ensure it is worth being part of your data architecture. Data has a cost. If it honestly does not have value, then it should be removed. Think about the 95th broken shell your child picks up on the beach and wants to take home because "This is pretty, too." You don't need to pick it up. You do not need to transport it. You definitely do not need to keep it.

Chapter 12

Data Lineage

Decisions are made on your data. If you have garbage data, you will follow that with garbage decisions. If you have good data and use it properly, your decisions will have a significantly better chance of benefiting your organization. It is essential to understand where your data originated and how the handoffs that contributed to its inclusion in your report or visualization occurred. The process of tracking your data from its origin through each of its handoffs, transitions, and transformations to its current location is called data lineage.

Data will travel from your source systems, both internal and external, through a series of procedures and processes to its current location in a data warehouse, data mart, data lake, database, spreadsheet, or file server. The data architecture is responsible for setting up, managing, updating, and verifying the integrity of the data through those handoffs. The data architect and governance committee are responsible for ensuring that data is properly defined, extracted, cleaned, transformed, and stored according to the needs of the users of that data. The definition of data changes as it is transformed. Communication of the new definitions to constituents is vital to properly using and interpreting that data.

Data lineage provides a step-by-step history of your data, including the origin of each data element, the transformation process, and the location where the data is stored. Properly defining your data's lineage allows your organization to better understand the data's journey throughout its lifecycle. A flow diagram can visualize the movement and transformation history of your data.

Your data architecture should include data flow diagrams for your most crucial data sets as a minimum.

The source of data

Where your data originates may dictate your data's quality, bias, and reliability, thus influencing your business decisions.

Data used by employees can come from many sources. Users might create the data. This is considered primary source data. Users might use data directly entered by other users or company machines into your systems. If your systems of record have strict parameters for creating data, as well as robust data governance that defines the meaning of that data, the source data will have better integrity and less bias based on the user who created it. This internal data can be dirty if you allow users to take shortcuts when entering the data or if user education is not enforced.

Your data may come from outside your organization, such as sources like social media, the federal government, the Internet, or partner systems. This is considered secondary source data and requires periodic checking. This outside data can be useful, but it should be handled carefully when making decisions. Data sourced from outside your company can change meaning over time, especially when the leadership of those sources changes. Keeping up with the changes in the meaning of external data sources enables you to properly extract data from the sources with the correct, current meanings. Understanding the biases and filters of external data sources enables you to identify and adjust which sources will influence your decisions.

Between the first two years of a recent global health crisis, the World Health Organization, along with many governments, decided to change the meaning of how people died. They simply changed the word "from" to the word "with" so the data would fit their narrative. This changed the inherent meaning of the available source data provided by those agencies. If your company pulled data in year zero, the data in years one and two would be very different. If your company relied on that public data to make crucial decisions, you would have very different resultant decisions based on the year's data you chose to follow.

When using social media sites as a data source, you must exercise extreme caution. The way social media works is to show content that appeals to the user. The material needs to be fresher and more engaging to make the content more appealing and thus keep users on the platform. The easiest way to achieve this is to gradually make it more extreme. This means that the feed you are receiving will gradually contain more biased information, whether politically, socially, or economically. This will not provide a reliable data source to help you make informed, balanced decisions.

The content of social media companies is subject to threats from politicians and the influence of source funding. Data presented on their platforms can be limited by political factors, black-box algorithm biases that match the views of upper management or developers, or funding sources. If more money is given to show "Post B" over "Post A," then your data source might improperly be filled with "Post B" posts, when "Post A" posts are actually more prevalent. There is a global historical precedent for this to occur. Remember that social media companies are, first and foremost, businesses seeking to generate revenue.

Another issue with social media data sources is the presence of content biases. Reviews follow Pareto's Law, better known as the 80/20 rule. 80% of all reviews are made by 20% of the users. If those users have biases towards your products or services, you will not gain a true understanding of your customers' voice. Furthermore, many companies will employ outside firms to generate thousands of reviews, making it appear that the product is better than it actually is. Again, using social media platforms as your main source of data should be approached with caution. You need to establish standards based on statistical principles and industry best practices.

Setting up standards for data lineage

Understanding the source of the data flowing through your systems is important. As we stated earlier, data that was trustworthy in the past may no longer be trustworthy or have the same meaning today. Sometimes, we don't even know the origin of the data we use or why we follow a certain standard.

You need to have procedures in your data architecture to vet and verify your data sources. You should have a clear understanding of the major standards used by your industry for data exchanges. You should ask if the standard you are using is the one that is best to use for integration, integrity, scalability, security, and analysis. Usually, standards exist for good reasons, but make sure they are the best ones to follow.

There are many standards for data lineage. There are several reasons to utilize these standards, including proper metadata management, compatibility, security, granularity, integrity, interoperability, and, most commonly, compliance with government regulations.

Standards set by government regulations

- **HIPAA (Health Insurance Portability and Accountability Act).** Deals mainly in the healthcare sector. HIPAA requires tracking protected health information (PHI), which includes how PHI data is created, transmitted, transformed, accessed, and secured. When your company undergoes an audit, a clear record of data lineage is often required to ensure data privacy and security.

- **GDPR (General Data Protection Regulation).** Requires organizations to maintain records of processing activities, which include the lineage of personal data. Compliance with the GDPR involves demonstrating how data is processed and moves through systems.

- **CCPA (California Consumer Privacy Act).** Similar to GDPR, the CCPA mandates transparency in data handling practices, which includes clear documentation of data lineage to demonstrate how personal data is collected, used, and shared.

- **Personal Information Protection Law (PIPL).** China's comprehensive data privacy law, which went into effect on November 1, 2021. It is often compared to the European Union's GDPR due to its stringent requirements for data protection and privacy.

With each of these policies, your business associates and third-party recipients of the data must also show their data lineage of the protected data. The standards include a requirement to show the full life cycle of the data you have for the citizens of each area. You must be able to trace the source, handoffs, storage locations, processing, sharing, and transfers of each part of the data. You also might need to show that you have only stored the minimum required amount of personal data for your pre-defined purposes and analysis.

Standards for metadata data lineage

The Dublin Core is one of the most used standards when dealing with metadata. Its strengths are in its four key characteristics of simplicity, flexibility, interoperability, and generic nature. The Dublin Core states that you should hold 15 core elements about your data:

- **Title.** The name of the resource.
- **Creator.** The person or entity primarily responsible for making the resource.
- **Subject.** The topic or content of the resource.
- **Description.** An account of the resource.
- **Publisher.** The entity responsible for making the resource available.
- **Contributor.** An entity responsible for making contributions to the resource.

- **Date.** A point or period of time associated with the resource.
- **Type.** The nature or genre of the resource.
- **Format.** The physical or digital carrier of the resource.
- **Identifier.** An unambiguous reference to the resource.
- **Source.** A reference to a resource from which the present resource is derived.
- **Language.** The language of the resource.
- **Relation.** A reference to another resource.
- **Coverage.** The spatial or temporal scope of the resource.
- **Rights.** Information about rights held in the resource.

Since all data can have these characteristics, data is easier to understand and implement.

This standardization makes the use of the data more flexible because the interaction of the elements allows for multiple combinations. This also makes the data more interoperable with other systems, as the standard is well-known and widely followed. As the elements are relatively generic, the use of the metadata is more versatile as well.

ISO/IEC 11179 is an international standard that provides a framework for representing metadata to facilitate the correct and proper use and interpretation of data. Consider it as a blueprint for creating and managing a metadata registry. The principles guiding ISO/IEC 11179 are standardization, data understanding, data sharing, and data quality. It provides a data lineage roadmap and guidelines on how to source, store, transmit, share, and secure your metadata and base data.

OpenLineage is an open standard for collecting and analyzing lineage metadata in data ecosystems. It defines a generic model for capturing lineage data, enabling interoperability between different tools and systems.

CDISC Standards (Clinical Data Interchange Standards Consortium) standards are used in the healthcare and life sciences industries to ensure the standardized capture and exchange of clinical trial data. These standards include guidelines for tracking the lineage of clinical data from collection through analysis.

W3C Provenance Ontology (PROV-O) is a W3C standard that provides a model for capturing and representing provenance, which is also known as source data, information (including data lineage) on the web. This standard can be adapted for internal data lineage purposes.

Standards for ETL and data integration

Your ETL tools, by definition, change the data. This transformation is part of your data lineage. It may be important to capture versions of the data throughout the ETL process. This includes capturing timestamps, user interaction, and internal processes at each step of the process. This processing of data is subject to government policies, security requirements, and storage requirements. As you choose your ETL tools, consider and plan for these potential pitfalls.

As you integrate or share data with other systems, standards for data formatting, data security, and data encryption are part of your data lineage. Storing this information will help when you are audited or asked how this particular set of data was obtained.

Your ETL (Extract, Transform, Load) tools used in data processing must adhere to standards for documenting data lineage. These tools should automatically capture lineage information as data is extracted, transformed, and loaded into different systems. The tools should automatically document and transfer that information to data lineage visualization tools according to your chosen industry standards and frameworks. Data lineage storage and visualization tools include Apache Atlas, Alation, Collibra, and Informatica.

Data selection

As you know, the sourcing of your data is important. If you choose the wrong sources, you will prove the adage, "Garbage in, garbage out."

What data you select to keep is just as important. Just because data is available does not mean that it should be saved. It is understood that storage is cheap, so saving data seems like the right thing to do. You need to realize the total cost of the data you save. With each piece of data you save, you are responsible for its storage, security, and use. Storing incorrect data that is later used can result in significant costs due to poor decisions. Storing useless data incurs a cost because employees must sift through it to find the information they actually need. This costs time and adds frustration to your employees. In the case of personal data, especially health data, you may become liable to a government agency simply by having a single data field that you cannot explain why you have it. The more data you store, the bigger the basket you need to secure and the bigger the target for criminals. You do not need to become a target for hackers because of useless data.

Knowing that storing data incurs a real cost, when extracting data from source systems for further analysis, you should be deliberate in selecting the fields and records you choose. Your data architecture should have defined the exact reasons and specifications for the data you will extract, transform, and load into your reporting systems.

The data governance team should do the data selection process, not the IT department. Representatives from marketing, accounting, operations, engineering, finance, human resources, management, legal, and other departments that provide and use the data should be the voice for selecting and defining the data. The data architecture provides the pathways for the data to flow and be documented, but the selection and desired transformation comes from the actual defined business needs.

It is very important to have the legal team be part of the selection and governance process. Marketing may want some information to play around with, but there is a difference between want and need. That difference could also cross over between legal and disastrous in the EU, China, California, and even your country. There might be physical location storage requirements for certain data sets that need to be considered when planning the architecture.

Cleaning and transforming the data creates new data by definition. This new data has new legal ramifications and new definitions. The data architecture needs to incorporate this aggregation, transformation, and change into the data lineage. Your ETL tools should enable the transfer of this metadata to your data lineage and visualization tools.

Your architecture should have an outline for the network bandwidth and computer processing power needed to perform the ETL process in a timely manner. This processing might be done locally or on cloud servers, but the plan for scalability needs to be designed upfront. This design should consider where the source data will be stored and where the analysis data will reside. There are costs in real money, resources, and especially time when moving data.

The timing requirements of the transformations and movement of data throughout the architecture help to dictate the systems your architecture will utilize. The data architecture design differs significantly when reporting is done annually or quarterly, as is the case for government reports and seasonal weather forecasts, versus real-time reporting, as is the case for stock market prices and live weather updates.

In many cases, real-time updates are performed by the system of record, rather than an ETL process. These live updates are part of the system architecture and, therefore, part of the data architecture; however, they may not have real-time ETL requirements. Your company needs to balance the cost of real-time ETL processes with the value of having that data available in real-time. Since there is a cost associated with selecting, aggregating, cleaning, transforming, logging each step in an audit trail, transmitting, and storing data, the selection of which real-time data actually provides true business value becomes a business decision.

Data architects need to possess the business acumen to recognize that "just because you can do something, does not mean you should do it." If there is a genuine business need, the architect should be aware of this possibility and establish the initial architecture with that requirement in mind.

Summary

When setting up the data architecture, just as with any system, there are the data needs and data wants of different factions within the company. The overarching data needs are your primary focus.

These are the highways that must run at full speed. Different contingents within the organization will claim that their wants supersede the needs of the company. If they are real needs, then the data architecture should be flexible and incorporate them into the highway. If they are wants, then they should be considered off-ramps of the highway. The data architecture should be flexible enough to allow these off-ramps to be processed to the side of the highway, and then the data should be brought back onto the highway if that data later becomes part of the needs of the company. The cost of off-ramp processing should be assigned to the contingent wanting that special service to compare it to the value of that data.

When dealing with the source, the selection, the transformation, and the timing of providing data, consider your data architecture as your global highway system. Ensure that your highway has cameras to audit the data as it moves through the system, allowing constituents of the data to track its lineage from source to analysis. Traceability helps with believability!

Chapter 13

Data Quality

What good is data if it's not correct? In the worst case, incorrect data can lead to incorrect decisions, resulting in adverse business consequences. The challenge of data quality is that it is a vast subject, encompassing many aspects of data and its environment. There is no single, simple definition of data quality. There is no one simple cure for poor data quality. There is no magic technology that can be bought that suddenly "fixes" data quality.

In the beginning, data quality refers to the accuracy of data values. For example, a person goes to the grocery store. The person buys some tomatoes at the grocery store. The price of the tomatoes is $4.99. The record of the purchase mistakenly lists the price as $4.79. There is now a difference between the actual price and the recorded price. The data has been recorded inaccurately. Regardless of who accesses the data or their specific needs, they will inevitably encounter incorrect data, and the person accessing it will assume it is accurate.

Structured data quality

Where, then, is the place to address incorrect data? The best place to address incorrect data is when the data is captured and recorded. The originating source of data capture is the most effective place to verify the accuracy of the data. If you try to correct incorrect data after it has been captured and recorded:

- You have lots of places to make corrections. Some of those places will be corrected, and some won't.

- You may correct one place and someone else corrects with another value elsewhere.

- Reports made before the correction to the incorrect data will not be synchronized with reports made after the correction.

Correcting incorrect data after it has been captured and recorded is futile.

An ounce of prevention is worth more than a pound of cure.

Data relationships

Not only is the accuracy of individual elements of data important, but data indicating relationships is also important.

Suppose Mrs. Smith places an order. Suppose the order taker inadvertently marks Mr. Jones as the person placing the order.

In this case, both Mrs. Smith and Mr. Jones will be unhappy. Mrs. Smith is going to be unhappy because she did not receive her order and Mr. Jones is going to be unhappy because he is going to receive something that he did not order.

The company making the mistake is going to be unhappy because they are not going to be paid. When a mistake is made in building relationships, the mistake has a ripple effect.

Other elements of data quality

Data quality extends well beyond the correctness of data. If there is any reason why a person cannot find and use their data, then that is as bad as having incorrect data.

There are a whole host of reasons why data may not be available:

- The system may be down and no one can access their data
- The system may be jammed with so many requests that a given query cannot be processed
- Only some of the data has been updated, leaving some data simply not in the computer
- The data may be in abeyance, waiting to be updated.

Textual data quality

Textual data adds context, referencibility, and "as documented" factors.

Text cannot be understood without context, and the context of text is woven into the fabric of the text itself. Context is often more challenging to discern than the meaning of the text itself. Yet, it is indelibly woven into the fabric of data quality.

As an example, consider the word "hot":

- Does hot refer to heat?
- Does hot refer to something that has been stolen?
- Does hot refer to a person's temperature?
- Does hot refer to a pretty girl?

You don't know hot's meaning until you understand its context.

The other element of data quality that comes with text is referencibility. Referencibility refers to the practice of showing the source of the text. On occasion, it is necessary to go back to the source of the text to understand its meaning and context.

Text also carries with it another element of data quality that is not found elsewhere: "as documented". What happens when a word is misspelled in a document? Suppose the word "judgment" is written in the document as "judgement," which is, of course, a misspelling. What should be captured in the textual database, *judgment* or *judgement*?

From the standpoint of linguistic correctness, it is likely that the word judgment should be included in the database. The author of the document did not write judgment. The author of the document wrote *judgement*. So, the question becomes, does the database analyst include what is correct, or does the database analyst include what was actually written?

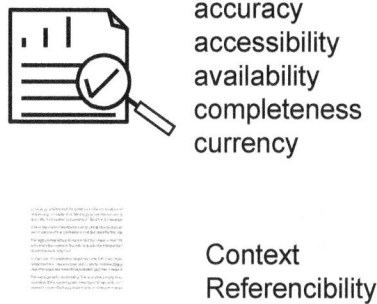

accuracy
accessibility
availability
completeness
currency

Context
Referencibility

Figure 47: With text came the need for context and referencibility in addition to accuracy.

So, it may sound strange, but in the case of text, the database should be filled with what the author wrote, even if it is incorrect (or thought to be incorrect).

The database analyst should not presume that he/she knows better than the author.

Analog data quality

There is yet another set of considerations for defining the accuracy of analog data. Analog data is data that is created automatically.

The issue with analog data is not the recording of the analog data (although that aspect is important), but the management of large amounts of analog data, most of which is worthless or worth very little. The primary issue with analog data is separating the worthwhile data from the data that is not worthwhile. This process is called distillation, which was discussed earlier.

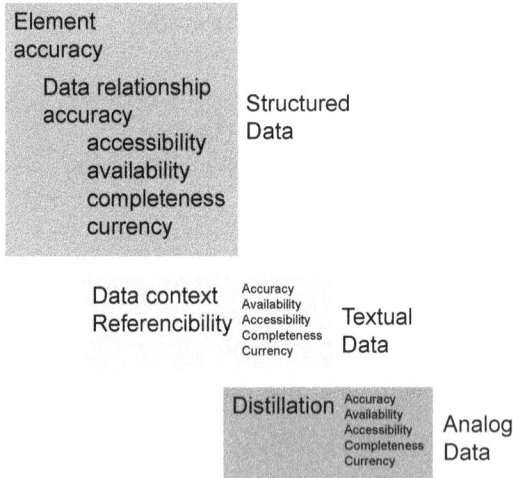

Figure 48: The evolution of data quality over time.

Summary

Data quality is a necessary ingredient for any foundation that supports new technologies. The very definition of data quality has changed with the introduction of new types of data.

Chapter 14

Data Believability

> *"If we have data, let's look at data. If all we have are opinions, let's go with mine."*
> — *Jim Barksdale, Netscape CEO*

Data used for decision-making must be based on certain fundamental principles. Good data must be simple, factual, accurate, traceable, timely, and, most of all, believable. If your data does not include these, you may consider using your employees' opinions. Bad data can be worse than no data at all.

Data must be simple

Data does not need to be complex to be effective. Some of the most effective analytics are based on basic data. Analytics need simplicity if you want your employees and customers to understand and believe them. Mean, mode, median, and standard deviation were all that were needed to allow Japan to overtake the American automobile industry in the 1970s and dominate through the 1990s. Deming, Juran, and Crosby showed this. Even Henry Ford and Sam Walton demonstrated that the use of simple statistics, charts, and data enables companies to become the powerhouses of their day. Timelines, bar graphs, pie charts, and heat maps are easy to understand. Make your analytics easy and trustworthy, and your employees and customers will trust your version of the truth.

Data must be factual

Just because someone claims something to be true, does not make it true. When data goes into your database, it should be what corresponds to truth. This is not a person's perception of truth but actual truth. Checks to verify the truth will help tremendously in making your data useful for decisions. Certain data can be verified as factual. Dates, document location, counts, current address, height, weight, race, payment amount, ICD Codes, blood type, marital status, and other measurable and categorical information need to be factual. Machine-loaded data should be factual but should also be verified periodically.

Systems used to source your data can have cross-checks to aid in the verification of facts. Using basic statistical principles, systems can determine if entered data is outside of control limits, allowing the person or machine that entered the data to recheck and ensure the data entered is factual.

Training employees on the procedures, necessities, and value of entering factual data correctly should be a part of your organization's continual learning plan. Entering the wrong data to "protect" someone's identity or feelings will cause more harm than good. It will lead to improper decisions regarding that person's needs and cause mistrust of all data coming from that source. Nothing good comes from allowing non-factual data to enter into your data architecture.

Data must be accurate

Accurate means factual at the time. Accurate data means the formerly factual data has changed and must now be updated. So accurate data has a time reference. Accurate data also has a level of detail reference. If the system records someone's age, weight, address, or marital status, that information can be factual and accurate at the time, but it may change the next day. Knowing a person's birthdate is more accurate than knowing their age.

Entering data that someone is injured is factual. Entering data that someone has a stress fracture to the lower femur is more accurate. Entering that someone lives in Kansas is factual. Entering the exact street address and apartment number is accurate. The factual data gets you started. The accurate data begins actionable decisions.

Accurate data may need to be updated over time. Factual data from the past may no longer be accurate today. For data to be accurate, the architecture should allow it to be updated to its current state while keeping the date range for the previous version. This leads us to the next principle of data.

Data must be traceable

Data lineage is the timestamped path that a piece of data follows from its source to its current state and location. This audit trail gives users more faith in the data they are using. They can trace the data back through its transformations to its source. They can see why it stands as it is today rather than how it was when it entered the system. Just like a piece of evidence in a trial, the chain of custody must be able to be defended for the judge or jury to believe in that evidence, data is the same.

Data must be timely

Timely means very different things to different people. In our world of instant gratification, real-time reporting has become an expectation instead of a luxury. Due to the nature of actual data needs, data storage, transmission time, transformation time, and associated costs, real-time data reporting is rarely required or actually possible. Providing real-time data ETL and analysis should be considered an off-ramp on the data architecture highway, but should be expected by the data architect as a constant request.

The data governance team, the data architect, and the data engineers should define the timeliness for the ETL of each data set. Many companies run a set of extraction scripts every morning to begin the ETL process. Standard ETL processes and flow timing are part of the data architecture. Proper planning of the timing for data extraction will help reduce stress.

Data must be believable

If the data does not follow common sense, it is tough for end users to believe what it says. Often, end users have a clear idea of what the data will reveal. They have a view of the truth from their vantage point. When the data does not align with their version of reality, they will attack the believability of the data instead of reevaluating their opinion.

A major retail chain had an extremely busy complaint line. The cost of employees overshadowed their profits. Customers were waiting hours to complain about products, deliveries, or experiences. They were irate when they finally managed to get through to the customer service representatives (CSRs) after their long wait. The viewpoint of the CSRs was that the company needed to hire more CSRs to decrease the wait times. This would alleviate some of the frustration that customers face every day. Their opinion was that the wait time was what made customers angry. This was their version of the truth.

A new director was hired for the call center, and they implemented new options based on the CSRs' recommendations. Expected wait times were communicated to customers, and an option for "a call back while keeping their place in line" was offered. There was no change in the anger levels of the call-in customers. So, interviews and surveys were conducted with customers. The resultant data from customer interviews directly conflicted with the CSRs' opinions. Customers were not mad at the long wait times. They did not like them, but the expected waits were communicated and mitigated. The real issue behind the customers' anger was not with the call center at all. It was with the unattainable "free" delivery promises made by the chain's website.

Customers were told they would receive "free next-day" delivery, but the warehouse did not receive the orders until the next day at best. Orders were delivered a few days or even over a week later. Customers were irate when they did not receive their products within the promised timeframe. The C-suite believed they needed to compete with other companies' delivery promises to keep their customers, but they never asked if that was possible with their current processes. The company could not.

So, the new director had the delivery times on the website reflect the actual expected maximum delivery times. Customers' buying habits remained unchanged. Despite the opinions of the C-suite, customers continued to purchase the same number of products from the company's website. What changed was the number of calls to the call center and the attitude of the customers who called. Complaints dropped by two-thirds. Wait times dropped to minutes. Customers called with more legitimate complaints and with a better attitude than before. The call center was able to reduce staff.

Using properly sourced data instead of opinions to understand customer loyalty and customer expectations allowed the company to rebound.

The takeaway here is that data must be believable for everyone. Your employees and your customers must believe it. If you, as the data architect, data engineer, data analyst, or data visualizer, use your data to lie, the adverse effect on your company far outweighs facing the truth.

Summary

As we discussed in an earlier chapter, it is essential to know the source of your data. Sources that initially appear trustworthy may evolve over time. As government administrations change, social media companies become political, news agencies become one-sided, and review sites change ownership or posting policies, your company needs to reevaluate them as valid sources of factual data. If your source is tainted, your employees and customers will lower the believability of the reports and analytics.

As your systems allow employees to enter faulty, inaccurate, incomplete, or unverifiable data, you may need to reevaluate the data that has been entered. Fortunately, your data lineage allows you to do this. If you notice that the data appears to be misaligned with expectations, you may need to recheck your security protocols to determine if intruders have compromised your data sources. In any case, the believability of your data begins with the factuality of the data source. Your data cannot be based on opinion or political alignments. It needs to be based on facts.

Chapter 15

The World of Analytics in the Face of Architecture

The primary purpose of any data architecture is to support informed business decisions. If your company loses sight of this truth, the costs will be devastating. The best and most consistent business decisions are based on the analytics gleaned from high-quality data. Good data is curated through a properly set up, business-focused, well-maintained data architecture. The architecture can include on-premises, cloud, or remotely hosted servers and platforms. It may include file servers, relational, node, graph, and NoSQL databases, data marts, data warehouses, data lakes, data lakehouses, data fabrics, data meshes, and API-based microservices. It may utilize vendor packages, homegrown systems, Lineage Auditing tools, AI, and ETL tools to coordinate, share, process, aggregate, and transform your data. The data architecture must provide a physical and virtual roadmap, enabling data to move seamlessly through the network. This is all for one purpose: Analytics!

Different users need to view the company's data from various perspectives to perform their jobs efficiently and effectively. This consolidated data, gathered and transformed from numerous systems, enables the creation of dashboards, reports, OLAP Cubes, knowledge graphs, ad-hoc reports, and drill-down reports that provide a comprehensive view of the company's performance. Analytics show employees where to focus their work for the day and pathways that do and don't advance the company.

Analytics and data mining techniques allow employees to see business opportunities in new ways, which may be the company's saving grace. Analytics used in conjunction with machine learning can maintain automated processes within tolerances and provide advanced warning when something requires human attention. Analytics in conjunction with Large Language Models (LLMs), Small Language Models (SLMs), Retrieval Augmented Generation (RAG) Models, and Generative Pretrained Transformers (GPTs), allow for efficiencies in writing emails and documents, consolidating meeting minutes, and understanding concepts from a different point of view. They also allow analytics through chatbots and Wikis.

Analytics with textual data enables employees to understand the voice of the customer, address areas of concern, and categorize the massive amounts of documents that organizations collect. Analytics forecasts customer and competitor behaviors by using historical data. Analytics covers a wide, ever-growing set of tools and services that give your organization a competitive advantage or at least allow your company to remain competitive. None of these analytics happen properly, using the right data at the right time, for the right purpose, without a planned data architecture and a solid data foundation.

Analytics do not exist without planned architecture. The architecture for a small company can be as simple as shared folders and some spreadsheets, but that is not scalable. Recognize that the need for a scalable architecture increases as your company expands. Plan for global competition from an architecture standpoint, and with your resultant analytics, your organization will have a better chance of forging that reality.

There are traps that data architects, engineers, analysts, and managers should avoid. Many companies have found themselves collecting data for data's sake. They fall into the trap that if we don't save it now, even though we don't know its source, validity, definition, or use, we may not have it to use it in the future. They are convinced by technicians that "storage is cheap" and we can just "transform the data for our needs after we load it." Companies often fall into the trap of "since we can do it, we should do it." Companies, just like people, think they need to do something because their competitors do something. We need to "keep up with the neighbors." All of these paths lead to waste. They are not good business decisions. They do not contribute to effective data architectural design. They do not aid in analytics. They are simply stupid decisions based on ignorance and arrogance. They are false promises for other companies to follow, but not yours! They erode a solid data foundation.

The root of your data architecture should be based on recommendations from an active data governance team and some well-managed source systems. The architecture should manage the data's ETL processes to your company's datamart and enterprise data warehouse. The architecture can utilize the immense power and promise of data lake technology if you can avoid temptation and utilize proper ETL or at least ECL principles as you load that data. Data fabrics and data meshes, along with the use of microservices and APIs, can enable the full realization of your data. However, understanding whether they are part of your data highway or part of your off-ramps is essential. These are not the highways. These are not the data foundation. You don't have to reinvent the wheel to create a great data architecture. You only need to use the tried-and-true wheels that already exist to build your competitive car. Always keep in mind that the primary purpose of all the architecture work is to establish a solid foundation to support your day-to-day operations, build your analytics, and prepare for future opportunities.

Index

www.ingramcontent.com/pod-product-compliance
Lightning Source LLC
Chambersburg PA
CBHW071415210326
41597CB00020B/3521

* 9 7 8 1 6 3 4 6 2 6 3 5 4 *